Now I'm Famous

An Autobiography by Terence Wallen

NOW I'M FAMOUS

Copyright © 2020 **Terence Wallen**

All rights reserved. No part of this publication may be reproduced, distributed, or transmitted in any form or by any means, including photocopying, recording, or other electronic or mechanical methods, without the prior written permission of the publisher, except in the case of brief quotations embodied in critical reviews and specific other non-commercial uses permitted by copyright law.

Published in England, UK, by DMJ Publishing
www.dmjpublishing.co.uk

ISBN: 9781671524897
Cover Design: Scale DM

Photography By: Creation Birmingham for Scale DM

DEDICATION

This entire work and those to follow is dedicated In loving memory of my dearest brother Sted Wallen, your love, inspiration and dedication has held me sure and steadfast whilst catapulting me to great heights, this one's for you, forever in my heart, forever in my pen (which has proved mightier and way more lucrative than the sword)...Rest Easy bro!

"Some people pass through our lives for a reason to teach us lessons that could never be learned if they stayed."

CONTENTS

Forward 7
Where the Journey Began 13
The Wallens 25
Evolution 47
Relationships 69
The Dark Days 101
Influences 117
Travelling 137
Accumulation Of Wealth 147
Giving Back 156
Acknowledgments 163
Staff 174
Useful Links 175

FORWARD

There is no known convergence of stars or cosmological coincidence aligned at the moment of birth that may indicate the path that an individual might take in life or the level of achievement s/he may attain. In fact, not even social psychology or geo-political references may assert with any degree of accuracy the fate of the individual. Yet, that an individual may attain fame may result from the collusion of space (where the individual is born or grows up), family values (the attributes, attitudes and outcomes of family members) and, in an intuitive way, chance or deliberate intrusions in the individual's life.

One such unplanned/unexpected intrusion was my first encounter with Terence Wallen, author of **Now I'm Famous,** back in 1977 when he was 5 years old. The little boy with shining eyes and a ready smile seemed to invite persons into his heart. Even then he exuded a sense of distinct purpose. There was something in the way he welcomed me, this unknown cousin from Jamaica. In a similar way he had welcomed into the family a year earlier his long-lost, late-to-be-known brother who had been left back in Jamaica as his parents moved to England to build their fortune. This brother, who was to become almost his alter ego, was Stedford Wallen, a.k.a. Worrell a.k.a. Calligan, to whom this autobiography is dedicated.

This autobiography defines and, at the same time, defies what it is to be famous. Like he has been all his life, he defines his fame and dares to assert it. With an almost casual candour, he goes through his life experiences – the good, the bad, the tarnished, the seemingly unimportant – and creates out of them all his definition of fame. Fame is him becoming well-known and even popular in a space where he might have been expected to be unknown. Fame is him being hailed as he walked by in the community when the passage of so many others is unheralded and unseen. Fame is becoming a role model for peers and those still unborn, to become a branded name that would inspire others to confidence. Indeed, to be famous for him may be, in the words of Rudyard Kipling, to be able to **"talk with crowds and keep your virtue/or walk with kings – nor lose the common touch**".

Terence Wallen defines fame and fortune for his peers and those others for whom his experiences will model achievement. It is well stated that our lives are made fulfilling by the extent to which we live for others. Terence Wallen has given his life to the development of others. He has worked with people living with HIV/AIDS and young people in sports and culture. He has remained a faithful member of his community and through it all he has been leader, role model, peer counsellor, and pillar of community development.

Terence's fame sought also to lift his family. He is tremendously protective of his mother and generously concerned for his siblings. And, latterly, on the passing of the brother whose shadow he lived in ironically as he cast his own personal shadow, he rose to continue his brother's legacy

by taking on unilaterally the community development project started by his brother which he supported over the years.

Finally, Terence Wallen's **Now I'm Famous** does not offer any psychological dissertation on fame and fortune, though these elements are to be found beneath the surface. It rather engages the ordinary in order to render it extraordinary, which he is. It is readable, usable, simulate-able material that young people everywhere may read and be inspired.

Sydney Bartley
Culture Expert and Consultant
Former Permanent Secretary/Principal Director of Culture and Creative Industries, Jamaica.

AN AUTOBIOGRAPHY BY TERENCE WALLEN

TERENCE WALLEN
NOW I'M FAMOUS

"Life takes us to unexpected places... love brings us home"
TERENCE WALLEN
#MYTRUTH

WHERE THE JOURNEY BEGAN

I was born and raised in Handsworth, Birmingham. I grew up on a key road in Handsworth, called Westminster Road, which is a prominent road that everyone knew about. We were a household of 10, in one of the biggest houses on the street. I was surrounded by older siblings and had only one younger brother. Where I lived was good, they were the best years of my life growing up. My mum was solid. She worked at the local school as a dinner lady, which I attended, which meant I always got a full plate of food, but it also meant that I always had to eat it all before I could leave. Could you imagine the shame of having to go back and finish your carrots and broccoli? And mum was not going to put on a show because she was at work, I'd get the same look and the same "Bwoy gwarn go siddung and finish you food, you know how much pickney deh a Africa a hungry" lol.

In the morning I would get up, my mum would make breakfast, Weetabix, porridge or simply toast on a plastic plate. I would then walk to Mark's house and have a cup of tea and some crackers. When I think of Marks mum, I always think of cream crackers. I would often be ready before him, and I would have a cup of tea and cream crackers while waiting for him downstairs. Then we would walk back past my house and get to the top of the road, outside the school and be crossed over by the lollipop lady, that was our daily routine. Mark's dad would sometimes drop us, but if he didn't, the rule was we had to hold hands, and we were not allowed to let go of each other's hands until we reached school. It was ingrained in us, that even when our parents weren't there saying "Unuh hold hands" we would get to the crossing lady, cross over and only then would we let go of each other. Like true brothers then we protected and looked out for each other.

In the evenings was playing out time. In those days I had one real friend, yes you guessed it, my same cousin Mark, he lived just around the corner from us. He was such a significant part of my childhood and youth, and I can't remember any other friends from the age of say 4. In those days, you only had one friend that could come to your house or one house that you could go to. I always remember, if I was let out of the house, I would go out of the front door, stay on the same side of the road, walk around the corner and to his house on Calthorpe Road, I was trusted to go to his house, and he was trusted to come to ours, it was literally an L shape path to take, with no roads to cross. We went back and forth in the scrumping days, the games we played were simply running and jumping over a stick, or running and jumping over a fence, collecting wood, building go-karts, rolling down his sloped garden or playing hide & seek in my garden and then we'd hide in the same places for years the game never seemed to get boring. Collectively Mark and I were the best at building go-karts from old pram wheels, planks of wood, old plastic school chairs, I'm not even sure where we got half of the parts from but when we decided that it was building time trust me we found all the materials and more. We had a massive big garden so we would run the go-karts down the garden, or behind some houses on Westminster Road was a long sloping back alley that lead from Putney Road to the back of the houses on Hutton Road, this was the ideal go-kart track, bike track, running track and even a strip for street parties, it was behind the Rasta House, home to Nyah Sound, so in summer they and other sound systems would string up and pump some bass into Handsworth. I loved those days, the Rasta's would look out for us and we would look up to them. On a good day Mark and I would get the chance to hold the mic and chat some lyrics ..."Oh lawd of his mercy mercy mercy puppa Terry inna di party party party" lol, you'd have to be there to see us in our short tailor made, 2 toned trousers with the flap on the back pocket, flared collar shirts and black pumps.

I even remember the excitement of being allowed to play out of the front instead of the back. We weren't allowed out of the gates at times, but you can see people walking or driving past. Our house was big, it was a 4-bedroom house with 8 children and my parents. I shared my room with my sisters as I was the youngest for 5 years, the golden child, the baby of the family...until my younger brother Wayne was born, then he was the centre of all attention, his round head got everyone soft and I was just another brother. Well that's not totally true....my loving nature, sweetness and broad smile still meant I was the special one. My eldest Sister Sonia was like the mum and the disciplinarian. She done everything at high speed, talk, cook, walk, discipline us, bathed us, dressed us, fed us and sent us to bed, she could do them all in one take. I recall when every one of us got chickenpox Sonia cared for us all like it was nothing, and yet she never caught it. Yvette was the softer one, the jokey one, the loving one, you could get away with more with Yvette than you could ever think about with Sonia. Yvette would cover for you, Sonia would lick you cross your head and still tell on you as if her punishment wasn't enough – no ramping about with her. After school, you were to pick up your book and get on with the work set by the teacher. I was so loved by my sisters; I was probably Yvette's favourite. She took me everywhere, by the time I was 10 I probably knew every Rasta House in Birmingham because of her. My experience of the Birmingham City Centre or even Perry Barr Shopping Precinct was as if I was in another city, it was a day out and I loved it, my experience being out with my sister Yvette would always end with a treat, be it chips, a Toffee Apple or Candy Floss, I loved when she'd say "I'm going out and I'm taking Tes". Both my sisters loved me dearly and that childhood love impacted on me ever since.

Once I reached a teenager, I was well in my own skin and a force to be reckoned with. I oozed self-confidence and made my presence felt everywhere I went, at times by just showing up. My school years was the best bloody years, my other brothers and sister Yvette had attended St Georges C of E , Newtown before me so the Wallen surname was already engraved in the school's history, but I was about to give myself legendary status over them and ensure I would never be forgotten. Ask any past student of 84-89 and 5years after because they'd still be talking about who attended the school, who are the legends? If my name aint mentioned they are haters or simply spent their whole school life in detention.

At St Georges, I had a solid crew. I had different cliques for different things, when it came to looking girlfriends it would be team Dean Sturridge, Terry Fleming, when it was time to cause chaos, get up to mischief and guarantee to be put on report it was back to Sturridge, Fleming and with the odd splash of Clinton Gordon and David Broombes. However, for consistent getting in trouble or being blamed when we were totally innocent the names Sturridge, Fleming and Wallen would echo through the school corridors. When in need of revision notes, getting my head down academically it would be team Ashok Bhopal, Gayle Martin and Avtar Obhi, there was a few others but these three I was already close to, the entire brains of the school, more than some of the teachers I think.

Outside of school I had a musical clique, there were four of us – myself, my cousin mark, good friend Curtis R.I.P and the female of the crew Gayle Martin. In my head I was the biggest Gregory Isaacs fan on earth, Mark was the biggest Dennis

Brown fan on earth, Curtis was the biggest Freddie McGregor fan on earth, and Gayle Martin was the biggest Frankie Paul fan on earth. Us four were huge lovers of Reggae Music, others around us, our peers, were all loving Hip Hop, Pop and RnB. We formed our own team as no one in our age group (11-16) was into reggae anymore. Everyday Curtis and I would meet up, and we would play music together either at his house or at mine. I would take my records in a plastic bag and go to Gayle's house which was in walking distance from mine, we'd chill in the front room of her mums house, records spread all over the floor and play track after track. Every time we got new records, we would meet up and have little sound clashes of our favourite artists. It was like having a private members club, our friends would ask why we were listening to old people's music, but it was significant to me, and finding people with the same passion for reggae music was something very important in our young age. It felt very niche, having people that understood my love of reggae in the '80s. We spent hours and hours playing 7inc and 12in 45 records and TDK cassette tapes. We used to record off the radio onto tapes, we even had the TDK chrome tapes, where the quality was meant to be better than the normal TDK's. There were no CD's, no MP3s, and no streaming music. I used to go to Don Christies Records, Bullring and Summit Records in town and buy my records. Don Christie was a white man doing reggae, he loved it and we loved him. Every Gregory Issacs record he would put to the side for me, I would walk into the record shop, and he would say "Terry I got something for you", and even if it was shit, I would still buy it, because it was Gregory Isaacs. In my bedroom at my mum's house, the walls were full from top to bottom of Gregory Isaacs posters and photos. I remember those days getting a new album and walking with excitement to Gayle's house to show her that my artist was still pumping out great tunes. I always thought deep down inside Gayle knew Gregory was way better than Frankie but her pride to this day won't bring her to admit it.

When Sted, my eldest brother, came to England from Jamaica, in 1976, he had brought a lot of reggae records with him, these included Gregory Isaacs and Dennis Brown, so the soundtracks to my life really began then. I soon became his favourite, and I began sharing room, time, space, thoughts and goals with him. That's when everything changed for me. He was an educator, he had a room full of books, I would sit in his room and read books, just being in his presence was enough for me. Music was the other glue that kept us close and together.

When I was growing up in Handsworth, Rastafarianism was big. I grew up in the era of sound systems. We had sounds like Lion, Nyah, Jungleman, Black heart, Rockers, Turbo Tronic, Stereo Classic, Now Generation, Romantic Bubbler, Orthodox and many more I can't recall but was responsible for the spreading of great music and introducing us to Mc's, Toasters and DJ's. As a youth, I was always around the elders, the Rasta's were very much a part of the fabric of the community, they were about peace, and I feel like I got some of my understanding of humanity, love and a peaceful livity from that time. My sister, Yvette, was a Rasta...well sort of, she wore the long skirts, diamond socks, Clarke's shoes and had dreadlocks under her wrapped head so I thought she was a Rasta but now believed she was a dread...significant difference , but being with her around Rasta's it played a major part in my growing up.

My mum wasn't the die-hard Christian, but she was certainly a prayer and a believer. With that said, we had to go to church. My mum sent us to Sunday school, and I was part of the Boy's Brigade. You learnt a lot of discipline in the Boy's Brigade, not just religion and Christianity, but also about being sure and steadfast, life skills, the uniform and presentation, around being obedient and a humanitarian. As part of the Boy's Brigade, you had to go out into the community and help, by doing things like sweeping leaves, helping the elderly, volunteering and delivering food parcels. You had to go through different stages and levels to achieve badges and promotion, by the time I left I was a Lance Corporal. You start at the beginning as a Private and have to work your way through numerous badges until you become a Corporal and then a Lance Corporal. As Lance Corporal, you are armband striped, you are a young person of authority, similar to a Sergeant, and you have jurisdiction over the young Privates that have just started. I was so proud of my gold belt and white lanyard, I ensured my gold buckle was polished and my lanyard brilliant white, my black shoes was mirror shine and id have a different kind of authoritarian walk once I had them on. Looking back, most of what I had to do in Boys Brigade i.e. looking after the elderly, going camping and learning to work as a team, all these things became my foundations. They played a significant part and became transferable skills that I continued to use growing up. Where I could have done much better academically if I applied myself more, I feel that my life experiences have equipped me well. The education of life outweighed my academic education, and that put me in a solid position as I learnt far more outside of school than I ever did inside it.

I went on to college, where I did my first diploma in business and finance. I then did the national diploma in the same area, which was made up of different modules, including Law, Accountancy, and Business. As additional subjects I did Sociology and Psychology, which I also passed. Even in my college days, I was already on the business wavelength, which I believe came from my brother, Sted. I was trying to follow in his footsteps as a businessman. He was a qualified accountant and all that I wanted, when I was young, was to be like him, and so I went to study business and went into business myself. I didn't go to university or get a degree. I went straight into work after that. While I was studying Law, I was on work placement at a law firm called Mandla and co, and the gentleman that owned the firm, Mandla R.I.P became my mentor, and that again, contributed to my life experiences outweighing the formal education route.

I think the education system today is very limited. It is structured and so limits what you can learn. It is very much geared towards the 9 to 5 working life, but there is a whole world outside of that. The formal education system does give a good grounding of discipline and learning, but in this new generation, people are being more creative. They are experimenting and focusing more on entrepreneurship or being self-employed, and I don't think the education system is aligned to that. I spent years studying French, History, and Geography. I didn't pass them. However, none of these subjects has applied to my life since I have become a businessman. I invested years in studying these subjects that I never use. When was the last time you used algebra or needed to know the square route of something? I studied it so hard to try and pass my maths exam, and I have not used it again since. I don't speak French, I can say bonjour, but that is it, and that's okay because most French people speak English. This is why I am not bothered if my child fails French at school. It is far less important now than it seemed to me back in the day. And as for history, let's not even go there, don't start me off on the education systems version on the 'History' we are meant to know.

Rasta, Church and Boy's Brigade, all made me mindful of the elders in the community. All the adults became like parents to me. They would look out for you and discipline you too. You would hide from being spotted by your mum and dad's friends because you didn't want them to tell your parents what you were up to, but you'd be just be scared of them collaring you like you were their child.

I had a great time in my growing up years, with great people. Doing activities like karate or going to roller disco's, they might not seem as fun now compared to PlayStations and Xbox's, but I was interacting and socialising. I wasn't sitting alone in my room with just the TV for company. I was out, around people. The roller discos were at Handsworth Leisure centre, and we went to Karate at Weld, off Heathfield road, both hosted by a community champion called Hector Pinkney – Known to many as Mr Handsworth or Captain Boogie. Meeting and interacting with all these different people are what I feel made our generation so solid as a group. The younger generation now is slightly more selfish and less sociable physically.

These are aspects that I feel I needed to have to become the man that I am today. Without these things, I would not have had the foundations to build on, so I attribute a lot of my growth to these experiences and great people.

AN AUTOBIOGRAPHY BY TERENCE WALLEN

"Some surnames speak volumes, this one is loud"
TERENCE WALLEN
#MYTRUTH

THE WALLENS

The Wallen's! It has a ring to it like the Soprano's don't you think? Ok perhaps not, but to me it's a dynasty within itself and if your privileged enough to be one or be born of one of the Wallen males and inherit the surname then your future is historically and genetically bright, destined for greatness.

Historically, I'm not sure where the name comes from. My Grandad - my father's dad, was Cuban, and my grandmother is Jamaican, so I think the name Wallen extends to somewhere in Cuba, but it could work its way back to Wales I heard, who knows? The surname itself stands for a lot in the current era. All of the Wallen's that I know, have been strong individuals, so the name means a lot to us as a family. It's like having a Royal Crest, we don't have one I don't think, but the name is symbolic like a crest. The surname means a lot, it really does, and the name gets bounced around all the time. When my kids were growing up, they would say proudly "Yeah, but we're

Wallen's though" I had instilled that pride in them from when they were young, you know we are Wallen's so there are expectations of us. In terms of the name being out there, Sted was the one that made our name solid in massive arena's. People refer to him as Sted Wallen, not just Sted. He was always proud of the Wallen's surname and encouraged us to be the same. Apparently we all have a look about us, the grandkids get it all the time, the Wallen features are strong and you can't hide a true Wallen, out and about I encounter elders who look at me with wonder and ask 'are you a Wallen?', and with a proud big smile I say "Yes, one is".

Mum

My mother's maiden name is Manning. She married my father and became a Wallen. My mother is without doubt the real core of all Wallen's. Small in stature but huge in her presence, her glory, her aura, her existence. My mother has and will always be the central bone where all the family comes together. That includes the children, grandchildren, great-grandchildren, great-great-grandchildren, cousins, you name it, they all come back to this one brilliant woman. NO matter how much the generations filter out, it all comes back to our mum. Her home is the epicentre of all of our beings. Every true Wallen finds their way back to my mother. Though she was born a Manning, she upheld the Wallen family name. My Mum worked as a dinner lady at the local Primary school, an iconic figure at Westminster School giving them over 50 years of impeccable service, never taking her annual leave and extended her role way beyond just dinner lady. My Mother was mentoring communities way before it was given a title. Many generations have passed through that school and knew her as Mrs Wallen or Ms Gloria. As we are such a big family, and there are so many Wallen's, and extended family members, carry us all is a magnificent achievement that carries some weight in itself. My mum was always the champion of the Wallen's. There will never be another solid strength like her, ever. It's impossible and we all show that we are incredibly grateful, and she is loved worshipped by all.

Pops

The Wallen boys took on some of our dad's traits. Some of us are sporty, outgoing, womanisers, into nice things and money, they're my dad's traits. He is sharp like a razor. No matter his age, he always looks sharp. He wears silk socks, his shoes are always clean, he wears dapper suits, open shirt, chain and the felt hat. My dad always put himself out there as a very sharp individual, and the boys will have carried on some of his sharpness and impeccable regards for presentation. My Dad has always been well travelled and encouraged us to do the same. I spent an awful lot of time with my father whilst he resided in the USA, we had a great relationship, we could reason, chill, share our differences. He has an ignorant side to him one of which I picked up but have worked hard on myself to rid myself of this inherited trait. Dad loved his parents, how you treated yours along with manners and respect was his standard by which he judged you. In my later years things became strained between us, we always amicable because I'm not raised to ever disrespect my parents. I have been independent of my Dad since I was in my teens, I really didn't need anything from him as such, I'll always love my dad, but I feel my biggest gripe is that I wish he would have done more for my mother. I only ever wanted him to keep her happy and watch them grow old gracefully together and for him to treat her like the Queen she is. I always had an issue with believing he didn't fulfil my wish. I'm a father myself so I know it's no easy task getting it perfectly right, accepting of ones flaws even as a father is something I've embraced and so wished he would.

Sonia

Sonia is the eldest sister. Looks like my mother, same height, same miserableness when she's ready. She is a true character and a half. I always remember her as being the mum when our mum wasn't there, and she is still very much the same to this day. She has a lot of our mums' traits. She is humble, quiet (When she not shouting from upstairs to shut her front door, get out her pots or get out her cupboards). She is the one who wants to make the house a home, cooking, cleaning and wants to be around her kids and grandkids, much like our mum. As a child she looked after us all the time too, I love my sister Sonia, she is something else when she is in her comedic element, jokes only she gets but you're sure to laugh because she is laughing. Sonia is as solid as a rock and the go-to sister for motherly advice, nurturing and definitely food. Oh, I forgot, Sonia is a human 'What's On', she knows of every Party (50s +), Christening, School Reunion and Funeral taking place in what would seem like a 100 mile radius lol, everybody loves Sonia.

Yvette

My other sister, Yvette, is the motivator. She will push you to do well, and she has done well in life for herself as well. She was born and bred here in Birmingham, but she moved to London and pursued a successful career. I was always her favourite little brother. From a child to a teenager I was always in her space, I was also the chosen babysitter for her first 2 children. She either paid me a fiver (which was a lot in those days) or rented The Gregory Isaacs Live at Brixton Academy Video and allowed me to watch it on repeat, knowing full well id be going nowhere once that was on. Of the 2 sisters Yvette is the jovial character, whereas Sonia is the more serious, Yvette is funny as hell. There is never a dull moment when she is around. The amount of jokes she can reel off, I don't know why she wasn't a comedian. She is funnier than me, maybe not wittier, but she is more amusing. Yvette can impersonate every single person she comes into contact with, if you escape being impersonated it's because she was too busy crying with laughter about somebody else. As a child as earlier mentioned I was my sisters handbag, I wouldn't be surprised if I hear a story of how I was tied in cloth in the shape of a bag and carried under her arm because she found it funny. Yvette took me everywhere with her, she introduced me to the whole Rasta scene and kept me under her wing. Yvette and I have always been close. A very sensitive individual, a worrier like my mother and looks very much like my dad.

Connie

My brother Connie is another character in his own way. He is quiet, calm, unassuming, hardworking and funny. He was a magician, yeah, real magic, not the ones you get in a lucky bag, He used to come to my primary school and perform various magic tricks like pulling a rabbit out of the hat and card tricks. He was a proper magician and part of the Magic Circle, which is the world's premier magic society. He can do illusions too. He is very intellectual, very smart, very bright and very intelligent. He is fantastic company and has a very good but dry sense of humour, you have to be quick witted to get his jokes. His jokes are much quicker than his driving, I've arrived abroad quicker than he has given someone a lift locally, he approaches speed humps with the same caution you'd approach a gun man. He is family famous for never getting a speed ticket or points on his licence for around 40years. Ask him for a lift I would recommend you pack a lunch and a change of clothing lol, love my bro Connie.

Ian (Stagga)

Third eldest brother is Ian, we call him Stagga (don't ask me why), he is the lyricist of all of us. If you're in a rush, you must only say one word to him, like "Hi". If you said "Hello, the weathers nice" he will bust into song lyrics, It will then turn into a freestyle, he will then start clapping the beat, in no time he will drop it like "Hello, the weathers nice, it nah rain, me need the sunshine to ease my pain and it will become a song and will in no time turn a simple 'Hello the weather's fine into a whole album and free DVD. I am sure he has about 50 albums under his belt, without ever having recorded or released one. I look forward to seeing him every Christmas because it has become a Wallen thing now, even the grandchildren ask "where is Stagga? When is Stagga coming?" just so they can ask him to drop some lyrics. He will protest at first and say "nah, nah, me nuh ready…" and we will say "Go on!" and he will say alright then and the next 10 hours of Christmas is spent just listening to Stagga He is actually a lyrical genius, he just does it for fun thou, something he has never taken seriously or as a career choice, but maybe he should, as he has some excellent lyrical content that could shake Up the reggae/dancehall industry not just my mums kitchen at Christmas.

Gary (Ringo)

Brother Gary. He is another hard-working individual. He is relaxed and very humble. You can sit down and reason with

Gary on several different topics. He is very knowledgeable about many things. He has a very calming nature and an excellent listener, he is not fussed about anything, he isn't driven by wealth or glitz and glamour. Very content with his blessings, an excellent father and sincere brother. He is happy to be alive and give thanks daily. He has a very strong religious sense. We could all take a leaf out of his book at times and do a little soul searching. He too is a lyricist but has actually released tunes. Very cultural in his delivery and a messenger through and through. We have a lot in common, yet we are so different.

Wayne (Bud)

Wayne is the youngest sibling. He was the last child. He came 5 years after me. I think I was meant to be the last child. There were shorter age gaps between the rest of the children, of around 2 years, but then came the 5 years between Wayne and me. He is also a very motivated young man, self-driven, lover of the arts. Similar to Yvette, Wayne is hilarious.

Very focused on a healthy lifestyle he is athletic, very fit and conscious about his body. He is very family driven too, and strong-minded. He is amusing, probably on par with Yvette when it comes to humour. He can turn most things into a joke, and he is good at doing character impressions. He can imitate anybody. If there is anything standout about you, he can pull it off to a T. he would imitate mums' friends, the women at church, the shopkeeper, anybody. It is a strength of his, he picks up on peoples voices, characteristics and movements very quickly and can turn it into a skit in no time. He is made for stage and the bright lights of The West End. Everyone says we look alike (well he looks like me because I'm older) lol....which makes him damn good looking, he has a more sculptured physique than I do thou, can dance better than me and can certainly sing better than I can....but that's all I'm giving him over me lol

It is good to have such a mixture of individuals within the family. Everyone contributes in their own way and brings their own input to a rounded family; these differences bring a good balance.

I do have siblings from outside of my parent's relationship, but they live abroad, and I don't know them well enough to speak of their lives or personalities. But the love remains and there is still time to build stronger ties and relationships.

I have so many nieces and nephews, some I am closer to than others, but they are all family and they all play a huge part. The older ones stand out the most for me. Daniel, for example, was my sister's first child, and the first grandchild. He was raised in our family home on Westminster road and lived there as the only child for a while. So, he would have gone through the initial old school raising and experiences we speak so proudly of. All my nieces, nephews, cousins etc even if they carry their fathers last name is still rooted in the Wallen legacy....and for that we all stand proud!!!!

Nathan

My closest nephew is Nathan. He is to me, what I was to Sted. When I was younger, I loved to dance, and Nathan was very similar. I kept him close to me when I was going out, I would take him with me. I can see a pattern, in each generation, we grasp onto one and keep them close. He had very similar traits to me, he looked up to me, in terms of how I dressed and how I carried myself. I had a love for watches and Nathan grew to love watches too. As he grew, we developed more common interests, like business ideas and events. It really does remind me of Sted and I. With such a massive family, you can't expect everyone to think in the same way or have the same approach to things, but Sted and I, and then Nathan and I, are very similar in terms of our mindsets, especially around business and success, I think that is why we gel so well. Nathan and I are business partners in numerous ventures and get on like a house on fire. He has a humour only he understands at times and that makes him all the more funnier. He will certainly be a success because of his determination, will power, drive and ambitions to change the game. He is a lovable character; everyone loves Nathan and he looks out for his nearest and dearest. The girls in particular love Nathan but that all I'll say on the subject because rumour has it, he'll be putting out his own serious of books on the subject lol.

I've actually lost count of the amount of nieces and nephews that I have, its actually pointless placing a figure on it as its subject to change by the time this is published. The males in the family can have kids by the blink of an eye, so ill refrain from actual numbers, perhaps it would be easier to give a between figure i.e. between

There is a lot that the younger generations of Wallen's may not know, so I feel it is essential to document as much as we can, so that they can learn, and find out about the history of the Wallen's and my mums journey and so on, be it through photo albums, books or videos. They are Wallen's within their own right, and I am sure they will make their own solid mark moving forward and they too will have a story to tell.

Disclaimer: Views and opinions of individuals are solely my own. If persons disagree with my views or opinions of them please close the book immediately, go buy a next copy of the book which my opinion of you has totally changed and you are mentioned in flourishing terms.

My Tribe

Shelika

I made sure I was going to cement more Wallen's out there and have my own children. Shelika Akhila Wallen, I named her, I think her mum wanted to name her after her nan or something, I shut that down real quick! My first child, and she is a proper daddy's girl with so many of my traits. If you didn't know I had other kids, you would think she was an only child. She is totally driven, independent, and has a great sense of humour. She is very feisty, cheeky and strong-minded, her words can beat the shit out of you, a no nonsense being. Anything that Shelika puts her mind to, she will achieve, she is a go-getter.

In the same way that I would always say I don't need a woman to carry me, as nice as it is to have a woman by your side, I can do this independently, Shelika is like that too. I'm going to give her mum some of the credit for that too, a champion of a woman, holds court and can be judge and jury. Shelika and her mother have exemplary mother and daughter relationship, I can't describe it no other but awesome.

Shelika is very much my backbone, she would eat you alive if you said the wrong thing about her dad, I'm perfect in her eyes, sometimes I have to wonder if she needs a new iris. I have been significant in Shelika's life from birth, at one point she lived with me, so she would have picked up a lot of my traits that way too. I was very strict with Shelika, and as well as very loving, I was able to find that balance. I was a strict dad; still kind of strict now but without the need to exercise that strictness because my boundaries are no longer pushed as she has grown into a beautiful mature Queen. I would pound in her head " Child you have got to do good at school, and you have got to get good grades" but at the same time, "I want you to enjoy life, go out there, find yourself, make mistakes and learn from them, always knowing Daddy will be there to cushion any fall. She would have picked up behaviours and traits along the way from me, but she would have picked up and learnt her own lessons in her journey too. If ever I was cloned, she is it, just with better hair quality and less filter in her delivery.

We will talk about the kid's mums later, as they are not Wallen's, I must stress that THEY ARE NOT WALLEN'S, though they might want to be, through marriage, it is never going to happen.

Jamel

Jamel is very much like myself, and he is the only child I had tattooed on me. When I had him, I was with his mum, so we were very close, solidly close. When a father has his first son, it's like "YES!". I knew he was going to go forward and carry the Wallen's surname and you can probably see more of the man traits in your sons, than in your daughters. Jamel is a very strong individual, we clash at times as we are so similar, in a lot of ways, like our directness, strong views and opinions on particular topics, we totally love a good debate and a healthy exchange in dialogue. Tall stature of a man, well-spoken and has a strong presence in any setting. I adore him and love him. One of the things I love about him is his love for his grandparents. He loves his Nan on his mums' side, and my mum undisputedly, you can see the love for them is ingrained in him. Regardless of where he is and what he is doing, he is always going to find his way back to his grandparents, which is beautiful. Jamel has a natural fatherly approach about him and consistently pushes his siblings to do well and remain focused. Jamel has King written all over him.

Keyon

Keyon - I have a very close relationship with him, I raised him well, perhaps spoilt him more than the others as he was a softer and craved more loving from the others. I can see a lot of myself in Keyon, he is another independent, hardworking young man, he doesn't have the same street knowledge that Jamel has, he has a softer side to him, this works in today's generation and I'm glad he's took his own route in life rather than following the crowd. He is more caring and content with being in and chilling with family than being out in large social settings, very laid back and cool. Towering over me in height his tall slim frame which predominantly comes from his mums side means he too can't be missed. Keyon started working from a young age, he always wanted his own money and was willing to graft for it. When Keyon was about 11, he was doing the gardening to make money, he would always ask for payment for chores, he had this entrepreneurial way about him, rumour has it he once set up his own tuck shop at school and was out selling the canteen at break and lunch times, he would buy popular items of snacks that the school didn't stock and sell them from his ruck sack. I never discouraged it, only said "if it true Son be careful of rules on school premises". I'm so proud of 'Shabba', that's my nick name for him, I called him that from he was child because of how he danced, now an adult ID call him Shabba for a totally different reason lol.

Teja

Teja is the princess of the girls, she too, is very independent and hardworking. She has had a very good life, but she remains very humble. You couldn't tell she has had a privileged upbringing, home and private school educated, so down to earth and grounded. Teja is very strong-minded, and she is very family orientated, she always wants to feel, be within and linked to the family. There is not much wrong Teja can do in our eyes lol and I think she knows it and milks it. She is a beautiful child to have, and she is so caring, she will give her last penny, she will stop to help the old woman in the street, that kind of humanitarian nature. Teja wouldn't want to pass the homeless man without giving him a few coins or returning with a sandwich and hot drink. I totally love her spirit. Quick witted, she will have you rolling with laughter. The lover of the arts and has strong creative edge about her. Like her mother she is also very business savvy and by the age of 16 had her own business, website, merchandise, YouTube content, you name it. It's impossible to not love this daughter I've been blessed with and share so much in common with. Daddy's little princess, thou she too will be taller than me soon.

Tenae

The journey with Tenae wasn't one of closeness like the others to say the least. A number of factors and external issues meant thou I was always present my engagement was minimal. Her mum and I didn't always see eye to eye, and it became more of an unbreakable friendship than a budding relationship, however a beautiful child exists, and the child has to be loved. Tenae was gifted with the commitment and time like the others, It is different because my other children were always around me, and raised around me, the relationship was solid with those kids, whereas Tenae was raised by her mother and Grandmother and I interjected where needed, the whole journey was different. Things got much better with time and as she got older, it didn't happen as early as perhaps it should have, but when it did happen, the love and the acceptance of Tenae blossomed into what now is a fabulous relationship. There is probably some resentment that she may feel from not having been part of the Wallen clan like the rest of the kids and that closeness she knows the others share, and I will just say that time heals. We try and make sure she feels part of this family and she has a good relationship with her brothers and sisters. I must take full responsibility for my lack of input, I'm happy that things have changed, and our relationship is full of daily love and laughter.

Having a slight strained relationship with her mother, coupled with the loss of her Grandma, Tenae rebelled and her cries for love perhaps wasn't heard whilst I was too engaged in raising my other kids, business and jet set lifestyle. I think a fear of the unknown, not knowing her well enough may of also played a part in my lack of early commitment.

It's hard to elaborate too much on how we got to this place, but I communicate with her literally every day and her smile warms me. She is full of fire, outspoken, takes no prisoners. I believe her and I are playing catch up, we both aware of the past and are now totally focused on the future. We still learning to get to know each other, her manners and approach to me is impeccable considering I hadn't done as much for her as I should. Try keeping us apart now…it's impossible. She absolutely glows around me and our relationship has had a favourable reaction to a number of parts of her life and growth.

Kayden

Kayden is my last child; I surprised myself when I realised his mum was pregnant lol, didn't know I still had it in me…, but he was a definite blessing. I saw a whole lot of changes in me when I had Kayden. The biggest age gap between my kids was before Kayden. The other children are 1 or 2 years apart, then a 5-year gap, then 2 close together, then a 12-year gap. I was 40 when I had Kayden. Kayden is such a Wallen, I believe he has every gene I have; he is just a blessing in disguise. It's great to have a child at that age, watching him grow, all the developments, from birth to teething to crawling to school. He is my biggest inspiration. All my other children are all grown up and independent now, he is the only one that is still dependant on me daily, so to speak. Whereas the others may depend on me financially or for advice, he constantly needs me, and I am always there for him. He is a loving child, with such a loving trait, he is so warm. He loves love, loves hugs and kisses. He is the child that while watching TV, he is playing with your ears. He wants to lie down and wants to sleep in your bed. It is beautiful, he loves being loved. He is a hard worker at school, I am very strict with Kayden, he understands my strictness. He very rarely gets out of line. I give him that look, and he just knows.... the balance is he is bombarded with love and affection. You have to experience his personality to get the true Kayden. He seems shy, but once he is comfortable with you, he will have you laughing all day be it with random dances, random jokes or random one liners. If I could have a virtual Kayden in my car with every day I would, be it school run at 8am or evening downtime at 8pm he is full of life and constantly wants to laugh, have fun, be loved and give love in return. Kayden is definitely a daddy's boy, his mum might disagree, but hey we know different!

So, there it is....

I may have other kids out there, and if I do, please come forward now, while I am financially stable and have a little life left in me lol. My children are all well linked to each other. Though at times, I haven't been a perfect father, I feel like I have done very well under the circumstances, I have balanced it well in terms of business, family and finance. I have been in all of my kid's lives and raised them the best way I possibly can. In areas where I may have failed them, they do not fail each other. There are no two kids that don't communicate or get on with each other. I set that up from the beginning, some are naturally closer than others, like Teja and Keyon – they are very close, in part because they were raised together, and slept in the same cot. They are only a year apart, and they lived in the same house. Kayden being the baby, he is loved by every grown child, and the interactions between them all are good, it works. Their mothers help me and make sure that happens too, that's a vital part of raising children. Especially when you are no longer with the mothers. All my efforts are into fathering, where I may have been a shit boyfriend, I totally refused to be a shit dad.

Now I am a grandad. Shelika, my first child has a little boy Kareem, so I have a grandson can you believe it, I'm a glam-dad, you'd never think by looking at me. It is not as hard as I anticipated, it's kind of easy work because Shelika is that solid as a mother, I felt that now I have got to be a parent again, but the reality is, I don't. Shelika is that independent and that solid, that all I have to give is love, and pass down some level of legacy. It's not about the finance or anything like that, it's just about making sure that he has an understanding of his history, his standing as a grandchild to me, and what I can pass down to him. Being a grandparent is fun, watching him smile, he is very young, and watching his mother just rock as a mother. That's my reward, I feel like I have done my job as a father, and her mother has too. It is vital that I feel like I have done enough, that the birth of a new generation, carries on some of the positives from my generation, and that they learn from the mistakes that my generation made and do things better than we did. I have told Shelika how time is more important than money, where I was so obsessed with being financially successful, my kids would have suffered for that. In your mind, you work hard so that the kids can get all of the things they want, but maybe some of the things they wanted were more time and not more material things. I want Shelika to make sure that time is the key thing, over the money, you can always make money and always survive. I am yet to see anybody, in my family at least, become totally desolate. I think we have enough brains to make money, and time is the only factor. I'm inspired that my children and my grandchildren make time to be a grandchild to my mother too, as she starts to age, the time you spend with her is valuable, and you have to make sure you get that time in with her over anything else.

Watching a whole new generation begin, maybe the hardest thing, harder than having to babysit, is making sure you leave a strong enough legacy for your children and grandchildren.

I don't plan to have any more children, but women like having children with me, so who knows. There is Peanut Punch, Guinness Punch, Magnum, Baba Roots to help lol. There are no plans for any more children though, it's time to just enjoy the ones I have and look forward to being a Grandad all over again when the others are ready.

"*It is not the strongest or the most intelligent who will survive but those who can best manage change*"

LEON C. MEGGINSON

EVOLUTION

Sopremes Night Club & Restaurant

When I was at the age of about 20, Sted had a way of doing things while keeping me in mind. Now there is a big difference between keeping me in mind and informing me. For example, he would decide that he was buying a property and that I was going to be the one to look after it, but without informing me. He did that with Sopremes Nightclub & Restaurant, West Bromwich. This was the nightclub to be in back in the day. It was black-owned, had 3 floors, a dance floor, Champagne Bar and a restaurant on the lower level. He casually came to me one day and said he had bought a nightclub that needs refurbishing, I thought it was a good idea, and then I realised I was going to be a manager of this big nightclub, that needs doing up, all whilst in my 20s. I was project managing the refurbishment one minute, working behind the bar the next or cleaning on another occasion. I had by now established a real strong work ethic and could do all aspects of the business, even change the beer kegs in the cellar for the draught beers,

I really felt in my element, I had to manage this huge nightclub, at such a young age. There were times I wouldn't see Sted for weeks. He had moved on to something else because he knew the nightclub was being taken care of. He was off in London or abroad somewhere. There I was managing staff, managing stock, taking bookings and everything else that comes with running a nightclub, while he was away. That threw me into the deep end, one of those scenarios where you just had to make it work. Part of my thinking was that I never wanted to fail him. I never wanted to let him down, and I always wanted to prove myself to him. I put my whole life into Supremes nightclub. That was a major turning point for me, managing a multimillion-pound business at such a young age. It was so time-consuming. When it was running well, in the good times, I could just be myself, in terms of my personality – meeting and greeting, people, you also realise how everyone loves you when you own a night club lol. The downside was when the doors were closed, and you have bills to pay, bookings to make, accounts to do, staff personality clashes, dealing with the brewery, etc. There are times when you are in your best suit, looking every inch the boss and the other minute, you're pushing barrels down the chute, cleaning toilets and changing beer kegs. It was a hard graft. The money was great, we were making proper money. We were THE club to go to, we were open every day of the week, we had daytime events, with massive Asian bhangra events, we did Soultime Tuesdays, Drum & Bass Thursdays, Bashment Fridays, R&B Saturdays, Big People Sundays, every day had something for someone.

Prominent DJ's like Dean Alexander had major events, plus a resident Wednesday club night, in those days to have names like Dean Alexander in your club meant your club would be getting national recognition because his following was huge. Imagine mid-week and the venue was rammed. Coach loads people would come from as far as London, Scotland, you name it, they would travel to be in Sopremes. Other big names that frequented the decks at Sopremes were Big John, Gauntie, Stevie G, and E Double D, Playboy & Chrystal force, Trevor Ranks, Wayne Irie, we had all the big DJ's playing at our club. It was the place to be. They had their own nights as they had such big followings. They were on PCRL and Metro radio station. Sopremes Nightclub was THE ethnic venue for the area. I went from boy to man there, it was there I met some great people and became close with many of the movers and shakers of that time. There were other venues mind you, all of which Sted or I would attend if we could to show our support. There was no sense of club v club rivalry. Many a night the owner of a club near the city called Porsche Club – Mr Vaughn Reid would be in our champagne bar rubbing shoulders with Mr Lloyd Blake the owner of the world-famous Hummingbird, whilst downstairs in the restaurant you would have Mr Verley who had owned Tabasco's Night club. We all supported each other, but more surprisingly they all supported a young me and for that I am truly grateful.

Charles United

Charles United was a football team I set up. We called it Charles United as Charles Road was where my mum lived, it was our HQ and where we all met up and had a kick-about before going to play football. Charles United went on for 17 years, and we worked with a lot of young people. We changed lives. Some of the kids that played with us have become professional footballers. For me, it was less about the football and more about mentoring. We got a lot of press coverage. We were on channel 4, speaking about how to deter young people off the streets and using sporting activities to reach them. Mentoring through sport was innovative at the time, we coined that method. We changed the lives of a lot of young people. We travelled and played against prison teams. It was about a lot more than football. As a local, 5-a-side team, we were securing sponsorships. Team members were given watches, and we had our kits made. We were taken to Wales to play against teams there. The majority of the youths that came through the team, I am still in contact with today, either as a mentor or as someone I support. We used football as a way to show discipline and commitment, we met regularly and had regular contact with the young people. Over 17 years we had many different people come through, some did great, some not so well, some ended up in jail. The key thing is that at that time, they engaged, and it was positive.

BSCD

The Birmingham Sports and Cultural day has been running for 21 years. It happens at the end of August in Handsworth Park,

Birmingham and was founded by Sted, he was the Founder and Event Director. At the time, I was the Assistant Director, but in his passing, I became the Director. That was another "throw in the pond" moment from Sted. I had no love for cricket, but he was doing the event and told me that I was the Assistant Director. He said he would take care of the cricket, I just had to make sure everything else happened. I did not want to let him down or fail him, so I applied myself, and 21 years later, I am still doing it. Sometimes I think, the way to swim is to prevent yourself from drowning. He used to throw me in, and I just had to survive. The event has always been significant to me, but now it is part of my brother's legacy, so now it is even more significant. I have my own team now; they see the same visions that I do. We have made some changes to how it was, but cricket still remains, and it is very much about him.

BRO-SIS

Sopremes was a lot about image and money. It was the fast life… but BRO-SIS was totally different. BRO-SIS was the most humbling success that I have ever had. It was about giving back. It came out of a simple need after my friend died. I was closer to his brother, who introduced me to him, and I began looking after him during his illness. I applied for a job as a support worker at Freshwinds. Within 2 weeks of getting the job, I spoke to the CEO, and I told him that I felt like I could do better than this, the type of service that they were offering, I didn't see any of my own kind there, but I knew they existed. I knew of one personally. I said I would find my own salary, my own team, and my own funding. I only asked that they let me use their building while I set up my own charity. He didn't have any African-Caribbean people either working there or accessing their service, so this was an excellent opportunity for him also. I spoke to service users and told them that if they knew anyone that was African-Caribbean that needed this service, tell them how good this service is for you, and it was very much word of mouth. Then the clinics began telling their patients about us, and that it was culturally specific for African-Caribbean's living with HIV/ AIDS and led by a young black guy who is from the streets. I have gone through clinical practitioner training, but that wasn't what was drawing the people in, it was my humanitarian side. My personality, my humbleness and my genuine desire to help was what got people to come and access our service. They wouldn't see my clinical side until later on, in the clinical settings.

We secured a lot of funding for this service. I was flying to Jamaica to cut deals with Slam Condoms, I was the first person to import them into the UK. I was the first person to start to put Afro-Caribbean images in GU Medicine clinics, before it was just white images, but now black people are represented. There was a different range of condoms available in clinics because of us, we were feeding into the hypermasculinity. You would see Durex, Mates – they were standard, but we made Ruff Ryders available, and that appealed more to the Afro Caribbean community. I also had a team that was second to none. They were probably the best team in the health sector at the time, in terms of numbers and delivery. Not everyone had a colourful past, I wasn't interested in what their CRB showed. I was interested in what they could do now. Past was left in the past. My team were solid. I poached a lot of them from other places, that were often nothing to do with sexual health, but I knew their skills were transferable. They were humanitarian, and they cared about people. I had 14 staff, sexual health works, drug workers, lay workers, volunteers, youth workers with a criminal justice element. We were in newspapers all the time.

We were invited to Jamaica by the government there to consult them on how to use the culture as a form of treatment. As an English youth, from the ends, having discussions with the Jamaican government on how to use culture as a form of treatment. The irony of that. That is our culture, but now I was there and introducing this concept to them. I was flying out and meeting with top doctors, and gynaecologist, TV personalities, the Prime minister, and they are all wondering where I am getting these ideas from. I was explaining that we already have this, and it isn't going to cost them any extra, they just had to employ the right people, who understood their service users. It makes it relatable.

I used examples that when we are sick at home, our mums give us soup, and while it may not physically cure us, it mentally helps us to feel better. So why in hospital, are the services users not given soup? Or something that they can relate to. They will look at their processed potatoes and not eat them; therefore, they are getting no nutrition into their body. If you allow them to eat their cultural food, it will make a difference to them. Even when it comes to the language - when you have someone from the African- Caribbean community that is in hospital, stressed out, and they cuss and say "bludclart, me wah this, me nuh believe in your bludclart tablet, them bumbaclart" their first response would be that he needs restraining, that they might need to call for security or the police. If someone understood his level of expression, and they were able to then put it into clinical terms, then he would get the right treatment. If you don't understand, you are going to be defensive and shut it down quickly. When I was in Jamaica and visiting hospitals as a consultant, in my 30's, I was helping them to make subtle changes, doing clinical audits. I was suggesting things like let's start off by painting. I got a deal with Dulux and shipped loads of paint over to change the colours of the walls, to more therapeutic colours, like lilac. I remember saying to one person in the clinics, "We all love God, but you have all these Jesus pictures up. It's like they have come to the end and they are about to go into paradise. Let's switch it around and ask the people what they like. Some people might like Bob Marley, so put up Bob Marley posters. Give them what they went so we are focussing on the living, and not preparing to die."

All these small changes made an impact. At the time in Jamaica, the focus was very much on caring for sick people. My approach was to empower sick people to care for themselves and change their mindset. Instead of feeding them, we are going to go through the process of helping them feed themselves. Day one we put the spoon in their mouths, then they put their own spoon in their mouth, then they get a bowl. We went as far as having to plant their own fruit and veg. We started to dig up the hospital back garden that was derelict, and now the service users were planting their own food, and it was also part of their exercise, and it elevated their thinking. Now they have grown it, they wanted to cook it themselves and eat it. They stopped thinking about the fact that they were HIV Positives because now HIV wasn't the only thing about them. Now they were a gardener. That was the thinking behind it, and it worked. I did the same in Africa and was called to speak at the World AIDs Conference in Namibia, I was the youngest speaker out there. At the time, there was a lot of publicity about the Gay community and HIV and AIDs, and there wasn't much about the black community or heterosexuals with HIV and AIDs. We were the community with the highest diagnosis rate at that time, because there was that much money and information poured into promoting good practises in the gay community regarding HIV/AIDs that the gay community started to use condoms. The gay HIV ratings were dropping, but the heterosexuals weren't using condoms, and the ratings were rising. I pioneered that, there is no way I could have done this without my solid team. They were so reliable that I often didn't need to go into the office. I had Maxine, Stephanie, Saf, Phillipe, Tawanda, Ezerine, Talib, Ryan, Darryl, Jermaine, Annette, Jason and Nathan. There is no way you could get a team as good. To this day, I am solid with each of these people. We changed the face of sexual health. When I left BRO-SIS to work for the BBC, it came to an end. It served its purpose, and it changed many lives. I once had a call from a hospital saying one of our service users was on the High Dependency Unit at QE hospital, which usually means people are near the end of their lives. I had never met her before, I went to see her, and she was very frail, and I sat and spoke to her in patois, and she kept crying. She reached into her bag and pulled out an old newspaper cutting of her son playing football for a team in Jamaica. She hadn't spoken to him in 10 years, I wrote down his name and who he played for. I went back to the office and contacted anyone I could in Jamaica to find her son. I reconnected them, and that gave her a new lease of life. She came out of hospital and went on to have 2 children. She would come to the service users meeting and share her story. One of my service users went on to set up a very similar service in Antigua, that is still running to this day, and he is always inviting me out to speak and be a director. He has set up a charity in Jamaica so on one of my visits, I sponsored his centre there. That came from using our service, seeing the impact it had and being empowered to do the same for his community. The wider impact of BRO-SIS continues to this very day because we were about changing lives be it staff or service users, and that we did and did it well. My proudest achievement.

Vivid Solutions

Vivid Solutions was important to me and different to all the others as I was working for someone that I mentored. That was such a good thing that it made the papers. It was a game-changer because I had mentored Darryl, helped and supported him to become something in his own right, and he then employed me. Having the corporate connections that I had, that helped me push the digital marketing aspect. It was ahead of its time, working at a very high level. Darryl also managed to secure massive companies like channel 4, BBC, Fattorini, Cloud Coaching International (Tony Robbins) and they were all impressed at the company's standard of work. You would have expected it to have come out of a 12-storey high, glass office building. It wasn't big in size, but it was enormous in quality and delivery. It was also great for me to see one of my proteges running his own business. It brought it all home for me because for years, I saw myself as the teacher, and then I was being taught by one of my students. It was a game-changer for me.

Ill Finesse

I remember working in retail, and I met 3 of the 4-man group (Darryl, Jermaine & Daniel) at the shop I was working at, we weren't talking about music, we were just chatting about random things. During that period, I was presenting on a Cable tv show called Studio 13. This was before Sky so became popular, so it was a big deal. I was heading in to record one day, and the guys that I had met in the shop was in the recording studio room next door. It turned out they were part of a 4-piece rap group called Ill Finesse – Their rap names were Fingaz (Darryl James), J.G, Lil D & D.R, and after hearing the music they were recording I approached them about being on the TV show, as we were looking for young up and coming talent. I spoke to my producer, I told him I had met this group, I liked their music and wanted to put them on the show. My producer OK'd it, so I got them to come in. They came in and did a live set on TV, and really impressed the TV crew. I kept in contact with them and, knowing I had had some management experience with my previous partner, I also approached them to become their manager. They were highly skilled, but they had no structure, and they needed management. I don't think they ever agreed that I was going to become their manager, but it happened. I was their spokesperson, and I was going to lead them to success. I think they were about 10 years ahead of their time musically. The individual skills between them were what made them so good. Between them, they had producers, rappers, writers and instrument players, and you don't usually find that in groups. They were now a young group, of skilled individuals, with a management structure bringing it together, it made ill finesse stand apart from any other young group at the time. I started to get them bookings onto shows, they supported famous UK artists such as So Solid Crew, Ms Dynamite, Artful Dodger, Damage, Mis-Teeq and so many significant acts up and down the country. Their lives shows were different from everyone else, they had dance routines with female dancers, props, they would ride onto the stage on bikes. At one point they had a live band that they played themselves. They stood out and were marketed as being more fun, they all dressed the same, with matching jackets from America. They looked a like a rap version of Jagged Edge or Boyz II Men. They used to rehearse at my house. I gave them keys to let themselves in, and they had to get there and rehearse every day. My most memorable moment was when they did an event called "Your time to shine" as I was part of it with Errol Lawson and Joel Blake. They smashed that performance and had the crowd screaming for more. I am proud that I had an impact on 4 young people, who then had an impact on many others, through music and teaching and many other things. We were offered record deals with big companies, like Warner Bros. So, though we didn't become successful in terms of a massive group, every individual became successful in their own right, and shared that passion and joy with others moving forward. That was a big part of my life.

BBC

The BBC wanted to come into Birmingham to do some consultation with young people around sports and inclusion, I do not know who told them that if they were coming into Birmingham to consult with young people, the person they needed to speak to, was me but I got a phone call from someone at the BBC. That phone call led to a meeting, and they asked me to be involved in organising a football tournament, voluntarily. I was happy to be associated with the BBC, so I said yes. They asked me to get some teams together, and I totally over-delivered. They asked for 4 teams, I got 40. They asked for 5 volunteers, I got 30. They asked for 4 companies that may be interested, I got 10 sponsors. By the time I had finished that project, I had received a phone call from a big shot at the BBC, saying they were sending me a train ticket to travel to London and meet them to discuss moving the project forward. When I got to the BBC offices and saw pictures of all these big faces on the walls, people like Terry Wogan, Chris Evans and Fearne Cotton. They offered me a job on the spot. Then I realised I would have to be stationed in London, so that was the first time I moved. Working at the BBC opened up a massive network of people to me. I probably met as many people, while working at the BBC, as there are words in this book. The BBC network is massive. I was meeting people in the corridors like Gary Lineker. My office was in the BBC Sport building, I would be in the canteen, and John Barnes would walk in, as normal as pie, carrying his tray and eating his food. It was very surreal. I remember seeing Rio Ferdinand and realising I was working around all these famous people, and it brought home to me how ordinary and humble these people were. I worked there for years, I started as a coordinator, and then I was promoted to progressions manager, ensuring the progression of projects and the young people in them.

I was involved in arranging their employment, training, and so on. It was massive and took me around the world. In my role,

I had exclusive behind the scenes access at the Carling Cup final at Wembley, where ghetto youth Terry, was now rubbing shoulders with some of footballs finest such as Jamie Redknapp, Alan Shearer and Didier Drogba. I met some of the greatest people on the planet during this time and had the most exceptional team. People like Caj Sohal, Dominic Cotton, Dave Verberg, Sahir Nadat, Mikey G, Tom Harvey, Steven Pookie, Lee Double, Harriet. I brought through a young girl called Larona Watts, she was a lover of women's football, and I helped her set up her own tournament called Brasilia, she did well in the BBC and got experience travelling too. Having the opportunity to work at the BBC and bring other people through, that meant a lot to me. BBC, as a brand, opens so many doors. I used to wear my BBC ID badge out, and it opened doors, people see the BBC badge and assume you are reporter, and they will talk, and listen to you. I was rubbing shoulders with the former Prime Minister Gordon Brown at 10 Downing Street, the power of the BBC is unbelievable.

A branch off from the BBC led me to Namibia, to set up the Pamodzi Cup, with my ex BBC colleagues Tom Harvey and Steven Pook, which was about bringing villages together through sport and then getting them treated for HIV/AIDS by immobilising Health Treatments to the people on site. It was a massive success and it's on my goal list to make it happen again.

Radio Club

While I was at the BBC, there was a lady called Helen Platt, and she was massive in terms of consultancy. Someone told her that if she wanted to do anything in Birmingham, that I was the gatekeeper. From then on, she was on me like a rash. She became like my agent. The work was pouring in, and Helen would ask if I wanted to do this or that. It was my first step into self-employment. Helen would put my name forward for all kinds of work, and through her, I worked for companies like shift, and we had the great photographer Finn Taylor, who became a great friend of mine. He has a vast portfolio. Working with famous people such as Wayne Rooney and Snoop Dogg. He has done the album cover for one of John Legend's albums. He is an absolute genius behind the lens. I managed to give him insight that he would not usually have had, like meeting gang members. Finn and Helen always empowered me and made me feel like Birmingham was my own, and no matter how big the project was, they made me feel I could do it. Even projects that I feared, like one called the Radio Club, it was a separate radio station for old people. I am used to working with young people, everything I have done up to this point has been aimed at young people. This project was working with the elderly, and I found that daunting, but Helen said I could do it, that my charm would get them. She told me that if I can get the hardest of the young people to listen to me and follow my dream, that the old people would love me. We made these old people into radio stars, it changed their lives, we even did a live show for them in Handsworth Park. The elderly people were barely coming out of their house before, and now they are radio personalities, and people knew their voices. There was one man from Smethwick called Little, he became famous for it. People were outside his house and knocking on his door. I rocked that project, we got awards and a lot of funding, we employed Kyrah Clarke and Zara Sykes. Everything that I have done, I have brought someone through with me. It was challenging at times but so rewarding and pushed my boundaries of ability.

Starlight Saturdays

Starlight Saturdays goes back to 2010, the first one was held at Smethwick Cricket ground. This weekly under 18's event was the brainchild of Nathan and I. I had really good connections with the authorities, in terms of the police and venues, and Nathan had good connections with the DJs and sound guys, so it was another great partnership between my nephew and I. Nathan came up with the name Starlight Saturdays, as he loved the tune "Starlight" by Dancehall artist Movado. It was the first under 18s Jam of its type. Normal under 18 events were just music, but our event was about mentoring through music, as a means to engage young people. It was successful, every Saturday afternoon, from 12pm till 6 pm, we went from a small cricket venue in Smethwick to using apache and then the Q Club, it was rammed every Saturday, the queues were all around the outside of the club. We engaged so many young people from inner-city Birmingham. It was a sight to be seen. We had a red card and a yellow card system, there were rules, even rules about the types of dancing we allowed. You couldn't put your hands on the floor, young people could dance together, but you couldn't gyrate, nothing provocative or out of the ordinary. We had security, no profanities, and all the music we played used the clean versions. We had great volunteers that ensured the event kept to our ethos, it was like Black Saturday school, but using music. We had the support of the police, of the local business and even a local judge. It was massive and went on for a couple of years. It got so big that we could not control it anymore, we couldn't keep up with the demand. After the event we used to have all the staff lined up outside like soldiers to usher the young people to their bus stops, members of staff in all of the shops on Corporation Street, supporting the shopkeepers and doing 1 in 2 out just so they didn't have 20 young people in their shop at one time. We made sure there was no extra cost, we had it all put into our proposal for when we met with the police and all the licensing agencies. They said it was the best proposal they had ever seen for a young people's event. We also used to have the Starlight Awards, where the young people that had done well in school, their school would tell us, and we would give out gifts and prizes such as football kits, balls and gift vouchers. We used to have funny awards, like best-dressed award, worst dancer award, fun things just to keep the young people engaged. We had themes like Nike vs Adidas, Bashment vs Soul, and so forth. From starlight Saturdays we birthed many great DJs, many great artists too; we had Jamelia, Trilla, Sykes,

Bugler all performing. Many of the artists felt aligned with what we were trying to do and embraced it. DJ Rem recently won the Young DJ of the Year award in 2019, and when he won it, in his speech, he gave credit to us for believing in him 10 years ago, which is absolutely fantastic. A lot of the young people that came through and were mentored are still doing well, we had people volunteer for us where they wouldn't usually volunteer for anyone. Some people had additional support plans, and I would see them during the week to go through it. We would meet them again on Saturday to have fun, but structured fun. We would stop the music in the middle of starlight to say a prayer, for our families and loved ones. We had indoor water fights; it was great. It was organised and well structured. I am yet to hear of another under 18's jam series that has been as successful as ours. We used to have 400 kids; violence-free and enjoying themselves. Imagine that. Every young person that came to Starlight didn't just want vibes, and a good time, they wanted better. We had time out rooms for kids that messed about, and a mentor would go in and speak to them to see what the problem was and how we could best resolve the issue. These things are lacking in today's culture, there is a lack of people using innovative ways to engage the youngsters. If you put on an event saying "Come and be mentored" Your probably not going to get the numbers in, but if you put on an event and sugar coat it with music, a safe environment, and then have several strong mentors there to engage with the young people, who can help the young people, you are on to a winner.

Elite Wines

Elite Wines is not my first dabble in commercial business, but this is my first dabble in a family-owned retail outlet. This was my nephew Nathans brainchild, and just like Sted would guide me but allow me the freedom to do it my way, I have done the same with Elite Wines for Nathan. All he needed was my support. It is the start of a chain of elite wines that will start popping up around the country. It has been very successful; it is a very niche service. It is one of the few alcohol delivery services in Birmingham open till 3am on weekends, in the same way, that you order your pizza, you can now order your wine. It is very much Nathans brainchild and business; I am just a partner in it. Similar to Vivid Solutions, I feel like I have come full circle. I used to employ Nathan, and now he employs me. That, to me, is a massive accomplishment for him, to see him grow and become his own boss, and he only needs me for my support, knowledge and expetise.

Creating leaders is probably how I measure my success.

Impact Solutions Group

Impact Solutions Group is probably a combination of everything I have done, under one umbrella. It is about social impact. It is about corporate companies, tapping into the social aspects and what you can give back. Through Impact Solutions, I have had contracts with Unilever, BBC, YouTube, Big Lottery, and delivered social impact projects for these major companies, which is what I do best. I am ensuring that smaller companies are benefiting from working with larger companies, or even just by using their products I ensure there are ways these smaller companies are getting something back in return, while they are spending with the larger companies who are already making millions. For example, Unilever has the largest selection of cleaning products on the market, and we did a project where we had them clean loads of community centres for young people. A simple project and it's giving back to the community. My team in Impact Solutions Group is made up of the same people from the past. I don't think there is a fresh face in there. They have the freedom to pursue their own dreams and goals, with the support of everyone else on the team and myself.

Those are the key business in terms of my evolution, that have changed my thinking or my stance in the community, and what I stand for in the community. These will be part of my legacy, someone, somewhere will have been impacted and inspired through these businesses, and so my legacy continues.

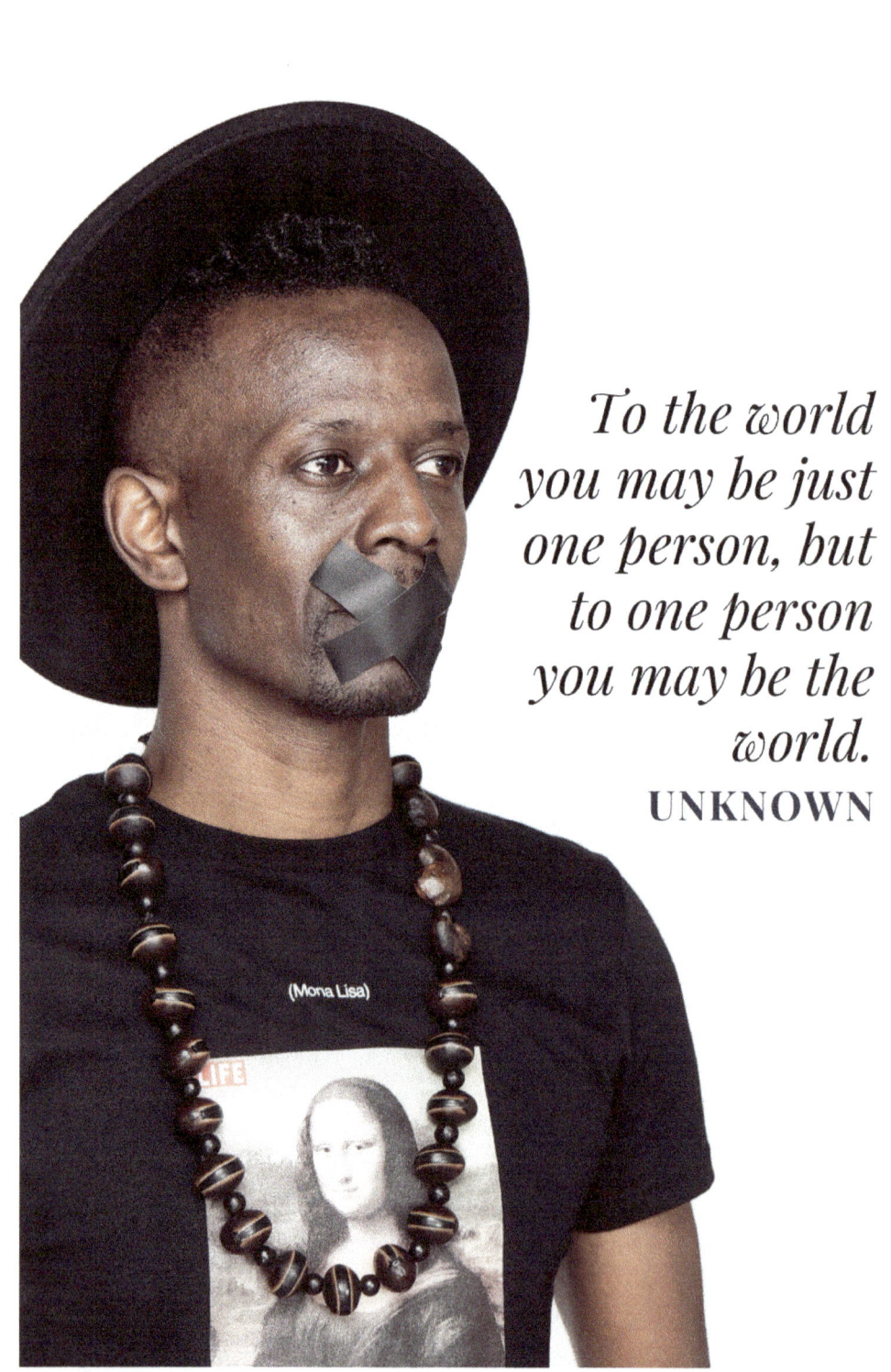

To the world you may be just one person, but to one person you may be the world.
UNKNOWN

RELATIONSHIPS

There was a singer, I think his name was Willie Nelson, that sang "To all the girls I've loved before, who have travelled in and out my door, I'm glad they came along, I dedicate this song, to all the girls I've loved before".....that's my song right there!!

I have had a lot of Girlfriends. Actually, a lot is probably an understatement. I have dated so many girls, I really have, many I can't even remember or purposely don't want too. But I can probably count on both hands, any that I have really, properly loved, and I that have had an impact on my life, seriously. My reputation, even from school days, has always been as a womanise. So that reputation has stuck with me, though I am certainly not the man now that I was then, as time goes on and you get more serious, you have more responsibilities, and you don't have the energy. Your back will go on some of these girls today lol. Things have changed, but if I was to think off the top of my head, about some of the women that have really impacted my life, these are the ones that are included in this chapter.

Michelle

Michelle and I started when we were very young, to be fair, I remember her telling me that I wasn't even her type. I was different from everyone else, I was about 16/17 and wearing suits to work, I had long camel jackets long after school hours. I was too proper, and I am not sure if that was the attraction, but I was certainly not her type. Somehow, she was attracted to me, she was and still is, this beautiful brown-skinned girl, she had her hair flicked over, she was nice looking. We got together, and it has been a great relationship then and even now. We have always been able to talk and communicate, it's one of her strongest points. I remember walking her to her bus stop each morning, that young love, waiting for her to come off the bus. We went to Handsworth carnival I remember being in a tent, listening to a sound system and standing behind her dancing, rocking left to right, aka whining out her rarse. I remember buying her a blue and white polka dot outfit, I must have been working at principles at the time and bought her this outfit to wear to a dance at Oaklands Birmingham and she was over the moon that one I could purchase an outfit for her, two it fit like a glove and three she was wearing the outfit of her dreams with the man of her dreams. She got pregnant with my first child Shalika, and we were solid. One time, we had an argument, "I said that is it, I am taking my child and going" and I got up and took her to my sister's house for a couple of days. I felt like yeah, I can do this. Michelle phoned and said, "I want back my child!" I said, "no, I'm keeping her!" I think my sister would have told me to give her back her child, Michelle would have known where she was, but I did take her and say I was keeping her. Michelle's solid, 30 odd years on and she still is my rock. She is a solid part of my life. I don't keep best friends, but she is like a sister, a mum, girlfriend, wife, all rolled into one. She is definitely ranked high up there. I call her Masha.

Annette

Annette is my son Jamel's mum. We went to college together, and we were very good friends. She was one of the lads, and when I got kicked out of college, she was solid. We had Jamel together. She is very grounded and mature. I'd say out of all the women; she was probably the most mature. She had her head on her shoulders and wasn't into what we were into, like when we were full of hype and raving - she was more inclined to stay home and look after her family, very homely, very educated. Annette was shorter than me, she used to have these classic finger waves down the side of her face, fair-skinned and tomboyish in her appearance. Annette would always have her jeans rolled up at the bottom with the latest trainers on. She was humbling for me, people probably wouldn't see how we mixed or gelled, but at that part of my life, she was what I needed.

I was living a fast-paced life, probably more money than sense, I was everywhere. Annette was calming, when she spoke it mattered. If I were contemplating going on a mad one, other girls wouldn't think twice about going along with it, but Annette would make me think, she would say "You have things to do tomorrow, you have college to attend, and this or that to do. She was a thinker for me, and I always needed that, she slowed me down. I can attribute my pace to her. If she hadn't slowed me down and influenced me the way she did, I think my life would have gone in a different direction. She had a calming nature that slowed me down. Later in life, I employed her to work at Bro-sis as she has always been so reliable and trustworthy. You can trust her with any and everything; money, business, personal stuff. You could trust her with the world. I take my hat off to her, she put up with a lot. All my crazy young times, dancehall times, all the fuckery and bullshit, Annette put up with it all. She has the same demeanour as my mum, she is very much like my mum. In her thinking, her behaviour, in the way she carries herself. If my dad was a wild one, my mum was never phased, she had stuff to do and got on with it, "when he comes home, he comes home".

Simone

Simone, I met her at Supremes nightclub. I think I met her through my cousin Ezra. We hit it off quite early. She fit my ideal type of girl, slim, tall, good shape, cockbottom, long legs. I always remember how quirky she was, even when she wasn't doing anything, she had a quirky, clumsy character, which was very attractive because that meant we were always laughing.

She would drop things; she would do things wrong while trying to things right. She couldn't dance for fuck, but the beautiful thing was that she would always want to dance, knowing that she couldn't. Christmas time, I would tell her to put on music, and she would try to dance and burst out into a funny laugh. We used to go to dancehall places like plaza together, the days of Spragga Benz. She could not dance, but she would bloody give it a try, and it made me warm to her. She is very ambitious and very independent of me. One thing I always say to Simone is that she can hear money from a mile away. If I put my hand in my pocket and rustle a note, Simone could say "that's a £10 note" she had radar ears, I could be in the bedroom counting money as quiet as I can, and she would be like "you counting money?!" I would tell her I was broke, and by the seams of the notes in my pocket, she could say "you look like you've got £50", and she was right. It was always an ongoing joke.

One of the things that I adore Simone for was that I had Keyon, and a year later, I had another daughter, Teja. Simone, without batting an eye, took her on, she also took on Shalika when she was 13 too, as she came to live with us. She helped to raise Teja, Shalika and our child together, Keyon. That's why Teja and Keyon were so close, they shared the same bath, the same cot. It was Simone's house, and she made a bedroom for Teja and Keyon to share, and then converted another spare room for Shalika. It is very rare to find a woman who is willing to take on a man and all his kids, and she literally did as all the kids were always at Simone's house, including Jamel. It's one thing to say yes, your kids can visit, but to say they can come and live there, that is different. Everybody loves Simone. Every kid loves Simone, and every baby mother loves her too. She has such a big heart, and she is funny. She helped me keep my kids together and plays a significant part in having my kids so close to me. I remember watching her in Tesco with a Teja in her car seat, Keyon in a sling, pushing a trolley, doing the shopping and I had to go there to meet her, and she was unphased. She always made sure Teja went to the same play scheme as Keyon in the summer holidays to keep them together. Teja became part of Simone's life.

Jem

After Simone, was Jem, another strong character. She was bubbly, had a beautiful smile, spring in her step, hair was always immaculate, and back then, Jem seemed really short. Jamelia was very cultural coming from a Rastafarian background, it certainly showed in her manner. She was just on the cusp of her music career, and it went so fast. I learnt a lot of new things during my relationship with Jem; meeting new people, touring, my understanding of the music business. It was hard to take on, I was sharing her with so many people; Managers, producers, even fans. It was hard sharing her time; she was always flying out. She was in London, and I would go every weekend or fly out to Europe to be with her, so it was very much me supporting her thing. The whole Jamelia thing was solid, strong personality, very independent, loving, caring, great mother, great sister, great family bond. She was very family orientated; I can't knock her. We had a grey area that became very public. I never speak about it, but I can say for the record, that I made some stupid mistakes. I was young and in a different place, different influences, and situations, my behaviour is not one that I would condone. In my relationship with Jamelia, I always apologise for what I have done wrong, but I will always stand firm around the things that were said, that were untrue. In the media spotlight, the papers run with what sells, and if I said it didn't faze me, that would be untrue. Having paparazzi outside my mum's house, it did get to me at times. It ran its own course, and there were times when Jamelia and I were cool, but the press was still running with their agenda. At times they would see Jamelia, Teja, Keyon and me out and about, happy and the very next morning there would be something contradicting that in the paper. I will not condone any type of domestic violence, with myself being a perpetrator of that, know that I did fuck up there. Fortunately for me, I learnt quickly and worked on the mistakes that I had made, I have apologised and spoken openly to my children about it, so they are aware of the whole situation. I apologise to Jamelia continuously, but we are cool now, she has let it go, and we co-parent our daughter Teja. It is not something that we still discuss. As a man, I put my hand up and say there is no excuse for that behaviour. I am not a product of my environment in that aspect as my dad was never a violent man, or physical to my mum. I have witnessed violence in my family, but there is no one to blame, but myself and I must take responsibility for it. It is a part of my life that I can look back on and think damn shit, that is not the way to go, and I can educate my boys on how not to behave, and educate my daughters on what to look out for and what not to accept.

When she released the "Thank you" song, my phone went mad, I was offered a lot of money to speak to the papers about the situation, the highest offer I received was £50k. Magazines and tabloid press were hounding me every day, and I would never sell the story. She is the mother of my child, my very good friend, I made a mistake, and it was pointless selling the story and dragging it on. Jamelia had the right to say what she wanted to say, she and I know the truth, so other people's perceptions don't matter. It did not affect me, my businesses or any of the things I was working to achieve. People around me saw me as the man they knew, not as the image the tabloids were trying to portray. I would go to a club, and I would hear it. I danced to it. I much preferred her song Superstar, that was definitely about me too (Grin). My daughter Teja is beautiful and educated, her mum is a fantastic mum. Jamelia and I don't have a bad word to say about each other, we co-parent, and she is very much a go-to person. In my times of need, she is there for me, and I am there for her. The kids see that and love it. She always supports me and my events, and I will always do the same for her. As successful as she is, as an artist, businesswoman, TV presenter, and she is very humble and grounded. To this day she always goes and visits my mum. It is beautiful when you have someone of that standing that fame and fortune to still be humble, grounded and normal. If you go to her house and say you're hungry, she will whip something up for you without thinking twice.

Latoya

There was a massive gap between Latoya and Jamelia, there must have been ones and twos but no one solid. I went into a food shop to get a Pattie and came out with a girlfriend. This girl was behind the counter, a nice Jamaican girl, she had the shape I like, slim, nice. I knew her sister and got on well with her before talking to Latoya. She was different from my other baby mothers, she was Jamaican born, where my other baby mothers are English born, so culturally she was different. She had different experiences of life growing up. Sometimes we clashed, I had to learn more about her Jamaican attributes. When you get yourself a good Jamaican woman, you will never go hungry, cooking, cleaning, setting your bath, taking the spots out of your face - all those things were next level. When a Jamaican girl loves her man, she LOVES her man. Before Toya, I was on a normal one meal a day. With Toya, I was on 3 meals a day and porridge. She spoilt me, and I was taken care of. She wasn't financially better off than anyone else, but her efforts would lead you to think she was. We had our differences and clashed in many ways; she has a temper on her. She did not stand for shit. My perception is, with an English girl, if you say to her "shut up" they would say "fine, it's your business, keep it moving" but a Jamaican girl is not taking that, she will argue back "who yu ah chat to? Me yuh ah tell fi shut up?" they are naturally confrontational and don't back down. So Toya and I clashed along the way, and because I was so used to English girls, and now I met this girl who would not take my shit, she would step to you and not let you run your mouth to her, and she isn't going to wither like a flower in the corner. Toya got pregnant with Kayden, which was good for us both, and made us see things slightly differently. She was still pregnant while she was studying business and admin at college. She is also very independent and a good worker. Between us, we were never going to have a lazy child, genetically, it was not possible to have a child that would settle to be whutless. We were always going to have a strong, solid kid. It changed us as individuals, but it did not bring us closer together, I think it helped us to find ourselves separately. We have our ups and downs, but we now work together to raise this wonderful son together. We communicate, but there are times when she blocks me, and times when I block her. It's sometimes whoever gets to the block option on WhatsApp first. It's funny because I don't have that relationship with anyone else, they can stop talking to me, but the gates are always open for communications. Toya may block me, but if I went and knocked on her door, she would still let me in. I also feel like regardless of her circumstances, I will always be there. She hasn't always had it easy, but she is still trying. I always say to her that I am one of her emergency services, she can always rely on me to be there for her. It's never going to be perfect, but we will always exist amicably, and she is a great mum, and I love her for it.

Natalie

I do not know what I was thinking when I met Natalie, that girl was as ghetto as they come. It would be like Prince Charles linking Cardi B. she was so ghetto, I don't know what the attraction was, but it was probably her bottom. She had thick legs and a good bottom. She had on white jeans the first time I saw her, and her bottom was broad. I remember saying to my nephew Natey, "who is that?" He said, "Uncs, that's MAD Nats." That should have been my warning, but I thought it couldn't be that bad. But it was. Natalie brought all her pains from her past into our relationship. She has had a journey and a half, and I empathise with her struggles and her demons, but I also applaud her strength and her character to pull through from where she has been. She also had to adapt to me, in those days I was the posh educated kid, she was the total opposite, not educated, not so posh. Dating me, got her out of sneakers and into heels. She gave up smoking, I got her off the road and back into education. Changed her image, changed her thinking, and changed her own thing. She brought so much pain and weight into the relationship; my shoulders were heavy with Natalie. Even though she was a bad gyal, she could cook like a grandma, she could keep a house like a grandma, she would feed everyone. She is the type of girl that the mans (guys) would link at her house, as she was one of the mans and she would feed every single one of them. Nothing was ever too much for her, if you said to her your sneakers were dirty, she would wash your sneakers, if you said you were starving, she would feed you. When she had Tanae, her whole life changed, my relationship with her, as friends, became much better. She is so motherly, if I called her for food, she will cuss me and run me off the phone but then phone me back in ten minutes to come and collect the food. She was integral to my life and very significant.

Bridge

If I was to go back to the beginning and puberty days, my first love was a girl I called Bridge, because she reminded me of Bridget Bardot, tall, sexy, beautiful top lip and strong. Them days she rocked the curly perm like a young Michael Jackson and had a distinctive gap in between her teeth which I loved. She was my first love, first erection; Bridge, first wet dream; Bridge, first everything else? Bridge. I was dating her at school, I was portrayed as a gyalis, all the girls loved me, and I loved all the girls, but Bridge, made me fall in love. When you are the man and every girl is after you, and in the chaos then there is one girl at the end of the corridor and the light is on just her? That was what it was like for Bridge. She was nothing like the rest of the girls, she stood out.

We used to do everything together, go for walks, watch films at the cinema and meet at the park. I would go to her house and sit outside on the wall for hours; she would come to mine and do the same. We were very much inseparable as a young couple. Holding hands, linking arms, meeting in the graveyard even. Who says there's no life in the graveyard eh? Beautiful times. She was my first love and my first heartbreak. In the end, she had to leave me as I couldn't hold down my womanising ways. For years after she left me, I begged her back. I told her I was going to change, she said no I saw you yesterday with someone. Then I would call her and say I love you, and I have changed, I am single. She would say she knew I loved her, and if I was single, we might meet and have a discussion then by the time we met to chat she would tell me she knows who was with. I just couldn't get her back. It developed into a beautiful friendship when we make eye contact, we know there is something there. Who knows, she could end up being who I grow old with and the person pushing me in my wheelchair.

We are great together.

Marie

Marie is probably my longest relationship, I was with her for about 10 years. We had our ups and downs. I fell for her beautiful eyes. I was madly in love with her, she was the first girlfriend that I travelled with. We went to Jamaica and San Francisco together. She was loved by my family, my mum, dad, brothers and sisters and cousins too. She was so humble. She wasn't hype or flashy, she was a good girl for me. I spent years with Marie, we used to be hooked on the comedy the Royle Family, and that was a great bond for us. She still visits my mum to this day. I found a new family in her family, Maxine, her younger sister, became my PA, my confidant, not my chef though as she can't cook for shit, but she became everything for me, especially in business. Her brothers, mum dad, and another sister have been a family away from family for me, till this very day. I still ask her brother Suthers for haircuts sometimes.

The Tune

I affectionately describe this woman as "The Tune", why? Because we have a particular 90s bashment tune that seems to have been the soundtrack to our relationship and every time we hear it then it brings us straight back to that memory.

Those days I was partying hard and so was she, we frequented most of the same haunts and it soon became a home away from home for us, actually music was like our release.

Back in those days, they called me 'Terry Bogle' ...famed for my great dancing skills after the late 'Mr Wacky' aka Bogle the famous Jamaican dancing icon. Not sure but I think she was smitten by my local fame lol. One thing I am sure about is that girl could drink, raaaaas she was 2 people. 1 was this beautiful young lady who would love me hard, keep my flat perfect, do my laundry, prepare meals and was so attentive you'd think this is going nowhere but marriage.....but then the 2nd person was always paralytic and had to be helped up many a stairs or taken home for her own safety. When she was sober (prob Monday to Thurs) she was an angel, come Friday she was possessed lol, I'm not even sure what her choice of tipple was back in those days but it was probably a cocktail of Thunder Bird, Steamers, MD 20/20 and Bacardi Breezers....(probably all in a pint glass lolol).

At this time I was living in a high rise block in Newtown, Birmingham, so thank goodness i was only on the 4th floor because if the lifts weren't working id have to carry her up the pissy, smelly concrete stairs. If you knew Newtown back in those days you would know the block of flats were not plush, piss was the new carpet on the stairs and in the lifts. Bwoy sah.....the struggle was real!!!

Skipping many many years on, you should see her now, daaaam, from that petite frame to now a well filled out sexy MF lol, be it jeans or dress it looks like its been painted on her defined body, that's either a perfect diet or the surgeon's knife, but who cares? Turn up the tune lolol. Never losing touch we tried dating again and it was beautiful to be back together again but as responsible adults, the circumstances weren't perfect but we gave it a bloody good go. Our issue I feel is that we are such good friends we always feared that dating again seriously may one day jeopardise the unconditional love we share for each other. I totally love this woman and now we have aged we've gone from 90s Dancehall to Beres Hammond and every time we now hear a Beres in the presence of each other, it's best we both leave out the nearest but opposite exits because like before the music has a way of drawing us back together.

What's also very funny about her is at times i have to wonder how music travels in reaches her and if we both hearing the same thing lol, i think at times when she's dancing her ears can ear the fine melodies of a classic Beres Hammond like "Now im falling, in love all over again, how could i ever doubt that you were my friend"...but her body would be moving to a dancehall tune like "Good P#@$y gyal fi get tings" lolol, i just couldn't understand it.....but i was not going to complain lol.

I don't see her often but we never lose touch via phone and our conversations are always fruitful, we can discuss our Kids, Families, News, Relationships, Goals, even peoples business lol, regardless what we discuss it never feels strained or forced and its obvious our friendship is cemented in authenticity, love and admiration.

My love for her will never fade and we will always respect and appreciate what we shared and what we now have....however it is to be described, very much the "When you know what you know, there is no need to entertain what they think".
We know the sound track 🎵🎵🎵🎵 (I know your reading this...if you listen carefully you can hear the music).

Ashtray

I dated another girl I will call Ashtray; she is a key friend of mine now, but at the time of dating her, we both wanted different things. When I started dating her, I felt like I had landed, I wanted to settle, but she wasn't there yet. That's when you feel that what goes around, comes around. Many times I had met girls that were ready to settle down, but I was all over the place, and then I met Ashtray, and I was so ready, I thought I am alright here, she was everything you could want, someone you could bring home to your mum, humble, kind, hard-working. She was everything I could want, but she wasn't ready for that at the time. That relationship didn't work out, but there is a lot to our relationship as friends now. She is possibly one of my best friends, and we communicate about everything, from business to relationships. She has been with me through my ups and downs, and I have been with her through her journeys too. We have an unchangeable love for one another and will always be there.

Nicole

Nicole was also another great girlfriend of mine, she had a heart of Gold, a favourite with my family, beautiful spirit and had a very calming nature. I fucked up there. If I had done the right thing, that relationship was marriage material, but I messed that up. We maintained a healthy friendship, but there was no Nicole taking me back.

Soldier Girl

I dated another girl that we will call soldier girl, or militant. Yeah, that sums her up. She has been a soldier throughout her life. I dated her for years and years, overlapping with everybody. It was never about sex for us, or about us being together. It was about our spiritual connection, which was very deep. It is a forever thing as far as militant is concerned, not necessarily as a couple, but our wavelengths are so on par, that it is forever. She is my homegirl.

Dancer

Dancer was Jamaican born but raised here. She had picked up more English traits than Jamaican ones, so she was easier to deal with. Dancer was a choreographer, which meant she was flexible in every sense of the word. The thing that stands out for me about her was that she was a freak in the sheets. Things that I didn't know existed, things that I didn't know about yet like being canned and whipped, this girl knew about, she put the F in Freak for sure. She must've been excited to be in this country and thought she would try everything in case she got removed. Lucky for me, she remained – thank you, Home Office, Thank You.

Eyes

There was a girl for the sake of this book we will call eyes, another strong girlfriend that I dated for a long time. She wanted me, she pursued me. I met her once while travelling back from London, on the Coach, and she gave me this look that said: "I am going to fuck you". We formed a relationship, and we had to travel to see each other. It was quite an experimental relationship, and we are excellent friends now - there is a pattern with my exes. I am sure if I were to call her now, she would be happy to jump back on that Coach and make eye contact with me again.

The Rasta Empress

Raaaaaaaas, The Ras, Holy Emmanuel I, Jaaaaaah Rastafari. Naturally beautiful, no makeup, no lashes, no nothing but melanin, average height, militant in her step, topped with an Okra and Dumpling body. Rocking a set of Map of Africa earrings, long well-kept flowing dreadlocks, smelling of coconut just as beautiful out as it is nestled under a khaki wrap.

This Empress right here is way too good for a man of the world like me! Her spiritual abundance can only be described as amazing. She so deep in her thinking sex was secondary to reasoning, plenty of times I wanted some Rasta hackling but had to settle for the burning of incense and discussing African art, but the pleasure of her thoughts was just as rewarding. A non-smoker of cigarettes but loved her weed, this would initially be a turn off for me as I don't usually date smokers, but as the true Empress she is she never smoked in front of me because "Her King nuh like it".

The Ras is an all-round winner in every department, understands men, always promotes the positive sides of Black Men, empowers Black fathers, you name it and if it's positive and about upliftment, she embraces it. Has a peaceful, calming, meditation-like aura, will make any King feel like he's on his throne!! Thou sometimes she pissed me off with her rambling because when she went in on me, there was no stopping, she would cuss for ages, I didn't just see red, I saw Red, Gold & Green. She always thought I didn't understand or appreciate her,

But……I wasn't ready to give up bacon, or a big mac, I couldn't give her the time she needed, I couldn't be the man she wanted or deserved to be honest, I'd have to grow a full head of locks n get rid of my dread Mohican, I couldn't live on soya, rice and lentils fuck that lol.

We are still cool to this day and she will always be extra special to me, when I decide that I'm going to move to Bobo Hill, Bull Bay, 10 miles outside Kingston, Jamaica, cut out the folly behaviour, get back to basics and let go of certain babylonism, I'm going to draw for her, get started on getting 11 kids (cos Rasta nuh deal wid contraception) and start my Rasta FC.

Kim

Then I branched out and went to Jamaica, then there was my Jamaican girlfriend, Kimoya. I met her through a friend of mine, at a birthday party over there. I wasn't interested in her initially, I thought she was cute, pretty and nice. We didn't hit it off straight away, but we were dancing at the party, and she was dancing with everyone, then she came and backed it up on me, Jamaican style. Even then I wasn't interested, I thought it was nice, but that's it. Then we exchanged numbers at the end of the night, we started to chat. Before you knew it, it was so good that I was flying back to Jamaica every 12 weeks. That is how much I was in love with this girl. Because I had previous experience with Jamaicans, and she was so different from the other Jamaican girls that I had known, I was drawn in quite quickly. She was in full-time work, had her own place, she was from the ghetto, but she was very clean and tidy, very ambitious and very driven. That was my first proper long-distance relationship, and I was making the real effort, and going to Jamaica as often as I could to see her. I really appreciate the effort that she made to make sure that even with the long-distance, I felt like I was her man, she worked to remove any insecurities I may have had. The distance was always going to be difficult, if there was ever any change in circumstances that meant I couldn't fly out to her, it could mean I wouldn't see her for 6 months, 9 months or a year. It isn't as easy for her to fly from Jamaica to the UK due to finances, the visa situation, etc. so that will always have an impact on the relationship. The times and distance allowed other stresses to creep in there. I remember her getting up at 5 in the morning and making breakfast or her being out on the veranda cleaning my sneakers, and handwashing my whites even though there was a machine she could use. The efforts she was making, I hadn't had before.

I am not knocking the English girls, but with some, I would be lucky if I got a cup of tea in the morning before I headed out.

Kemoya made every effort to make sure I was well fed, well clothed and looked after my house immaculately. We had a thing about co-ordinating our clothes. She would lay out my clothes for me, which I found beautiful. She would say to wear that white t-shirt as she was wearing her white t-shirt or wear the Adidas as she was wearing hers. It was so beautiful. She was not perfect, but she was perfect for me because I am not perfect either. My hats off to her and my first long-distance relationship.

Baby Shark

Baby shark. She came out of nowhere. She fits my profile; Pretty, tall, good shape. I was in a shop, and She walked past me with someone else one day, and I thought damn, who is that, and shortly after she walked past me again, and I thought I was never going to see her again. I saw the person that she was with about a month later, and I asked him who she was. It could have been his girlfriend for all I knew, but he said it was his cousin, and that was music to my ears. I asked him to tell her I said Hi and if she's around I'd like to see her again.

Coincidently enough I saw her walk by me again another day in the same shop (what's the chance of that), she was styling it out because I know she received that message and she was now walking by for me, but she was playing it cool. With baby shark, it is refreshing. She is younger than I am, she has Jamaican parents, so she has a lot of the attributes. She is ambitious, a trier. She tries really hard to accommodate and please, and she tries to be a man's woman. She tries to understand men. I think that's where a lot of women have failed, they understand themselves, but they don't try to understand men. She tries to understand men and why we do the things we do or how we act the way we do. She tries to counteract it by finding the thing in her that may make him want to change himself, rather than her trying to change the man. She does these things that make me question why I do things. Her efforts are very high, she is continually working to reinvent the relationships and trying to keep the honeymoon period for as long as she can, and I adore her for that. Some girls, you date them, and they change after 6 months, but baby shark keeps it fresh. She still keeps it fresh and tries, I don't just mean with food and those things, she is always trying. I also rate that she is happy to support any of my ventures, she always offers to help. She could easily just relax and live a luxurious life, because of the stage I am at in life, but she chooses to be part of the graft with me. As much as she enjoys having her nails done, she is happy for her nails to be chipped and break, to stay in with me and work through documents. Having experienced a lot of women, this effort really stands out. The reason I call her baby shark is that she is very soft and sweet, but she also has a bite to her.

Obviously, there are loads more girls that I have dated, some have not been mentioned in fear of being sued, others I just aint got shit to say about them!

AN AUTOBIOGRAPHY BY TERENCE WALLEN

"*Sometimes a good cry can cure what a good laugh can't*"

TERENCE WALLEN

THE DARK DAYS

Dark Day 1

The dark days make you appreciate the bright days. Without the dark days, the bright days wouldn't be so meaningful. Going through life, you should ideally have more bright days than dark. I have certainly had my fair share of dark days, in fact, dark days is probably too light of a description.

In 2007, there was a very dark period for me. I made some stupid mistakes in a relationship. That very mistake, which I am responsible for now, caused mayhem at the time. Looking back now, it doesn't quite seem as extreme, but when you are in it, it feels like mayhem. It brought a massive amount of stress and upset to my family, my friends and to myself. It brought a lot of grief to my mum, which has always troubled me. It was a very dark period. It opened up my eyes to some things around making dumb mistakes. In the end, it was resolved, but what I had done was split two families apart, not by myself, but I have to take responsibility for my part in it. We had enough foundations to bring it back in the end. We had meetings to say this was wrong, this should never have happened in the first place. If I knew then what I know now, I would never have made the errors in judgement. I was in a different place, different mind, different scenarios, but it was a harsh lesson to learn. In times of darkness, you know who is who and who your friends are. If I took one thing from that situation, it was that you will know who is there for you, who is real and who is fake. Who is there to say "yes you fucked up, but you are human, one bad year doesn't make a bad life" Who is your backbone and strength, those people who showed themselves then became my REAL circle. They have shown themselves over again, and that situation showed that.

If you can't stand by me at my lowest, you don't deserve to be by me at my highest. if you're absent during my struggle, don't expect to be there during my success

I'd say, through that period, Sted was always solid. It was a solidness of truth, he would blast me in private, and he would say "yes you fucked up there, but you are my brother, and I know there is more good in you than there is bad." Also, he was able to understand that during the whole journey of growth, that things are going to go wrong at some point, and not to judge on what goes wrong, but on how you can put it right and move on.

My nephew Nathan, was probably the closest person to me during that period. We are not of the same generation, but we were so close that we could speak openly. For some people, like my mum or Sted, I would have to water it down as they wouldn't be able to understand. Nathan took my heart in his hand, put it in his pocket, and decided that he was going to protect it, regardless of the repercussions. Going through the highs and lows with me. He totally proved himself, I had never doubted him, but he came through. I feel like Nathan is a clone of me, there is nothing I wouldn't have done for Sted, I would defend and protect him, and Nathan has that same trait with protecting me. My daughter Shalika was solid too. She knew the ins and outs, and she was very much the same as Nathan in helping me during that period. Everyone's understandings of things are different, so I can't expect everyone to respond the same way to things, but she was absolutely solid. My core team was Nathan Shalika, Michelle and Ezerine. They helped me through that dark time. They saw the truths and lies, they saw the light and the dark and they measured it for what it was. The downside of it is that I now have some broken relationships, and I have to accept that. People react based on their perceptions and experience. Some people based on their anger, misinformation or lies. It cost me some relationships, and some repercussions crossed into other family members lives. They feel they suffered for my wrongs, which was never my intention, but that is a lesson to learn – your fuck-ups can affect other people in ways you may not see.

It went on for almost 2 years, and the way we resolved the drama was to get around the table. We had interventions and mediation. We talked it out and today, touch wood, it is all done and buried. It will never totally go away; it will always be there in some minds as it was somewhat life changing.

Dark Day 2

Dark day 2 was not as dark as day 1. My second dark day was when I went through the whole Jamelia thing. My name and character were constantly tarnished. It affected me more when I saw it in the papers, seeing it on the news, or when someone would say to my mum "Is it your son Terry?" the newspapers were running away with their stories, it affected my children too. The main reason I would say Dark day number 2 wasn't so dark, was that, as they say - if you recognise your flaws, people can't use them against you. I had already identified the mistakes I had made, and people close to me were already aware of them in regard to this situation, so that meant I wasn't completely knocked for six by this experience. I think the darkness would have been more profound, and the cloud would have hung over my name and reputation longer. Though I must add, it never crippled my work, no one ever said they would not work with me because they had heard about Jamelia and me. Having my name out there linked to domestic violence is a low point for me. If I could turn back the clock, it is something I certainly never would have done. All these years I kept a dignified silence because I had to respect the mother of my child and her career. It is pointless trying to pass blame or judgement, when you know there is some truth in the story, it was not like the way that the papers glamorised it, but I had been a perpetrator of being violent to women. I totally regret and am ashamed of it. It is not how I want my sons to grow up, nor what I want my daughters to be on the other end of. I learnt a tough lesson from it during that time. It was a dark period, but I continued and persevered through it all.

Dark Day 3

My next dark day was in August 2017 when I lost my brother Sted. That was surreal. Sted died of a sudden heart attack, but I was blessed to be the one to find him. I could not prevent death, it's not within my powers, but me being able to be the one to find him, and to be able to be there for him at that moment, to hold him, and set him straight and make sure he was dignified by the time anyone else saw him was a blessing. Sted died the day before our Annual Birmingham sports and cultural Day event. I woke up that Saturday morning of the event thinking how come he had not phoned me? He usually phones me a hundred times a day for the stupidest things, and when you look back now, you can think, why did I miss his calls? There would be times I would see him call and think to myself - I can't be dealing with it now, he is just going to tell me to do something or ask me to meet him, I would always call him back later. He called me so much, I was like his conscience if he was buying shoes or a suit, he would call and ask what colour, what colour tie should I wear with it? Or he would call and ask me what I was going to eat. Even at my age, for my

Birthday, he would give me £20, and every Friday he would call me and ask if I wanted KFC. If he went to a Jamaican food shop, he would just buy me some food then call and find out where I was to get it to me. We did so much together; we travelled together, had businesses together. Losing Sted was a very, very dark time for me. I had to struggle with losing my rock. Towards his later years, I felt like he leant on me. I had leant on him so much in the earlier years, but I felt like with him passing while he leant on me, I also felt like, as his rock, was there anything else that I could have done differently that would have given him a better quality of life while he was still here. He wasn't sick, so he didn't have a poor quality of life, it was more thoughts like, could I have woken up earlier and gone to his house a couple of hours earlier that day?

Anyway, I had a feeling that morning that something wasn't right, I knew it wasn't right as he hadn't called me. The event was coming up the following day and he had called me on the Friday evening to meet him at the park, but I had told him I wasn't able to do it that day. Something was being delivered and I had been there before where I had been there signing off on barriers for example, and Sted didn't even turn up. He would call and say he was stuck in traffic, when it was 7 pm and no traffic, or that he was stuck in the queue at KFC as he knew I was hungry. But I wasn't able to go there that Friday. He didn't call me back after that, which is normal, but I knew that when I woke up on Saturday, he would call me first thing. When I woke, he hadn't called. I remember phoning Nathan and asking if he had heard from Sted and telling him something didn't feel right. I told him that I was going to go to Sted's house, and he told me to call him when I found him. Then I continued to phone Sted, but there was no answer, so I went to his house.

His car was outside, but he didn't answer the door when I knocked. I looked through the letterbox and went around the back. I thought this is weird. Sted always gave me a spare key to all his houses, even houses that I have never seen. He had said to me, the week before, "Remind me to cut the key for this new house" and in my head, I was thinking I am not going to remind him, I can't be having more keys. I had so many keys for him, and he would lose his keys and call me to drop keys to him all the time. I was now standing trying to get into his house, and I didn't have a key. Knowing my brother, and that he loses keys often, I knew there was a key somewhere around. I was searching under the bins, under the bricks, checked in the plastic containers in the back. I touched the ledge and felt a key, and so I put it in the door, it worked, but it was locked from the inside. That was the point that I knew something was wrong. I ran back to my car, got a hammer and smashed the door in. I was going through his house, calling out his name, and pushing open his door with my left hand, I couldn't find him. Where has this man gone and left his car? And his blue channel 4 bag that he carried with him religiously (it had all his documents in) was in the living room, along with the papers for the event that was the following day, and his shoes. Where has he gone without his bag, his shoes and his car is still outside? I stood in the living room, with my hands on my hips, thinking where could he be? Then I thought, have I checked every room? I had only gone through and slightly pushed each door while calling out his name and waiting for a response. I hadn't been looking inside the rooms for him, just listening. I remembered that the bedroom door hadn't opened fully. I went back to the bedroom, and that is where I found my brother behind the door. I pushed the door and pushed him at the same time. I was in total shock. I felt like I couldn't breathe. He was there lying down, and I could not breathe. I was saying "Sted, Sted", but he was already dead, and cold. His hands were grasping near his heart. I came out of the house, still not being able to breathe, I went out trying to catch my breath. The first person I called, before 999, was Nathan. I later asked Nathan what it was that I said, and he told me that all I did was breathe and pant Sted's name. After that I did call the ambulance, telling them what had happened, they came quite quickly. They came in and opened his shirt, but it was too late, he was already dead. I was in total shock, consciously trying to man up, telling myself to get myself together, but it knocked me for six. The ambulance makes you sign for ownership of the body, as they don't take dead bodies, they're there to save lives, which you don't think of at the time, when you sign to take responsibility for the body. What I wanted was for my brother to be in a dignified state, so I wanted to put him back in the bed, I lay him down and put his hands across him with a blanket over him. I was trying to make him look nice. The ambulance guys had contacted the coroner and asked if I was ok. Then I had a moment, I am not sure what happened, but I lay down next to him on the bed. When I found myself again, I was in the same position I had laid him in. I had my feet on the bed and face to the ceiling, I don't know what happened in those moments, or how I got to that place, I think I may have fallen asleep, but when I came around, the first thing that came to my mind, was that I had my shoes on his bed. I had on some red Adidas, so I turned to the side so that my feet were off his bed, and then I was facing him. It was that moment that I felt like I had slept and woke up. It was interesting that the first thought was that I had to respect how my brother has raised me and take my shoes off his bed. You cannot put shoes on a bed. He would take off his shoes when going to any house. I was facing him and talking to him, out loud, and I can hear him answering me. I am having a conversation with him. I put my hand over him and kissed him, thinking how cold he was. Then I fell asleep again, because the next thing I knew, there was a knock on the bedroom door. It was the coroners, and they woke me up. I remember telling the coroners that he and I were not ready. They left the room, and I just lay there and hugged him.

At some point, I got up and called Shelika and told her and Nathan to come to me. Everyone else, I told to go to my mum because she would hear the news and she would need everyone around her. I knew I could handle this here, so they needed to go to her. I'd called his daughter's and informed them too. Shelika's mum drove her to me at Sted's, and we held hands, forming a circle, with Sted also, and prayed. That was when I felt like he was ready, and I told the coroners that they could take him. Then I made his bed because I knew he wouldn't want it left unmade.

We then went to my mum's house, by that point she had already heard the news, and she took it like a soldier at the time. She was in shock. Sted was the man of the family, he replaced my dad 10 times over, and he set a standard for us. We all looked up to him and were proud of him. He was far from perfect, but he was perfect for us. He had left us, and he was gone, just like that. I threw myself headfirst into the planning of his funeral, and that is what kept me afloat. It kept me going. At this point, I hadn't grieved, and I was running on autopilot, planning the funeral with the help of family members, but it was very much my thing to do. I became very selfish, and there were constant arguments and breakdowns in the family, looking back now, some of it could have been avoided, but I was selfish to the point where I felt like no one could deliver his funeral better than I could because no one understood him like I did. I didn't feel like anyone else had the drive to get the standard that I wanted for the funeral, I wanted it to be perfect, like a state funeral, one that he deserved. Throwing myself into the planning helped me, I had to be strong for others, and for myself as I knew I had things to do. We brought his daughter over from Jamaica. There were a lot of mixed emotions; guilt, anger, sorrow, laughter when remembering "if Sted was here".

After the funeral, it became totally black for me. Looking back now, it was because I had nothing to do. My job was done. I spent days in my bed, I did not have the energy to get up. Every day was a crying day, every day was a dark day. I felt sad and depressed. I kept seeing him, I think I fought so hard to get the last image of him, of finding him dead, out of my mind. I felt like I was going mad because I was constantly fighting that image. I lost weight. I had people calling and seeing if I was ok, but I think at that moment, I needed to be around fewer people, not more. That often happens when someone dies, at first everyone is around, and then after the funeral, the numbers slowly go down. There were times I felt like I was going to give up, I couldn't see how I would get through it without Sted. I was never suicidal, but I couldn't see how to carry on. I used to get up in the morning, I would keep the blinds closed, and found myself talking to myself in the mirror, trying to psych myself up, I was saying "Come on Terry, listen, let's do something today, let's get out of the house. It's what Sted would have wanted." And then all of that would just end in tears, and I would go back and lie down. I just could not do it. I realised that this wasn't me, and decided I was going to go for counselling. I felt like I had to get help. I had buried him on 6th October 2017 and went straight to Jamaica, I thought it was going to be the best thing for me. In truth, it was the worst thing that I could have done. All the photo's that I took while in Jamaica, you can see the sadness in my eyes. I look dazed and had no smile. I felt detached and away from home. When I came back after 4 weeks, I started counselling. That helped, as it allowed me to say how I was really feeling, to someone I had never met, and there was no judgement. It is hard to talk to the family when you are grieving, as they too are grieving and because of the family rifts, I wasn't even sure who I could talk to. I had trauma and bereavement counselling, and it helped. It was a dark period for me, and it will always be difficult. I am still doing Sted's annual event, it's hard because he chose that date. He died the day before his event, so when I carry it on, it is so close to his date of passing. Last year it was on the exact day.

I am not yet 100%, but I am motivated. I am motivated to make sure his daughters are doing ok. I am trying to be there for his 3 daughters, Chantelle, Chanel and Alanna

I'm committed to the things that really matter, like taking my niece to her prom, which I knew Sted, would have done as her dad. I am flying out in February 2020 to celebrate his other daughter's sweet 16th party in Jamaica, his eldest daughter is getting married, and she has asked me to give her away as he is not here. The fact that she asked me, while there are other brothers, has that sense of me stepping into his space as the one to support them, and hopefully, be as good to them as he was to us. Using all his teaching and guidance over the years, I hope to match all the good that he brought into the family and to the people around him. He appears to me sometimes, I didn't believe in that before, but I do see him. I have seen him walk by my bedroom door and once I saw him in Handsworth Park.

I want to say that it is ok to be vulnerable, it is ok to cry and to breakdown. I am very much a showman; I carry myself and walk with strong positive energy. It is ok to be vulnerable, you do not always have to portray this strong, untouchable guy, who laughs every day and doesn't cry. This process helped me understand that, and it has made me a better person. The hyper-masculinity goes out of the window on the dark days. Also, it made my friends and family, who thought they knew me, know me better now, as they have seen the softer side of me now, not just the joker side, or the businessman, they see another side, a vulnerable side. Which I have never had to show before. It is alright to be vulnerable and show weakness. Weakness is nothing to be ashamed of. Hopefully, someone reading this somewhere will understand the pain of having been through it, and or when they may go through it, they will seek the correct help and be helped through it.

My friend Sacha really helped. We phoned each other many times, and she has a great listening ear. Sacha was a rock and still is because she knows I'm not yet totally out the dark place. What was funny about Sacha is that I'd always think she has a 6th sense because she would always seem to know when to call. Our spiritual connection meant she was informed every time my happy level dropped. It's truly amazing the deep connection you can have with someone. For her I'm truly grateful.

My daughter Shelika had me on suicide watch it seemed, she was on the blower a million times a day, checking where I was and what I was doing. I got that every day for months. I can only assume she saw something in me that I didn't see because she was very protective at that time. I thought I was coping but it seems I wasn't , I've never asked the likes of Michelle or Ezerine what they saw of me during these times, but I know I must of been well low for Michelle to invite me to come live at hers whilst I go through the process. You can hardly get an invite for a cuppa or to sample her now famous Salmon much less being invited to live in. I love my team unconditionally.

It affected my mum a great deal and seeing my mum in so much pain, hurt. She speaks about him every day. Any time I go there, she talks about him the whole time, and sometimes I can't bear it. I know it is good for her, and it's her therapy, but there are times when I don't want to hear or think about him, in a nice way, I am not there yet, I am not in that frame of mind. She is tough though, and it is tough to deal with. Death takes people from you, and it brings people to you. It definitely takes people away, not just those that passed, but some that are living, because it shows you who is who.

While writing this, my Birthday has just gone, I went to the graveyard as I felt like I wanted to spend my Birthday with Sted, though I didn't get my £20 from him lol. I went and sat and chatted with him. I can still hear his laugh, and certain Dennis brown songs that I play, remind me of him.

It is tough on the family, but we will get through it. It has pulled some of us apart, it attributed to some family breakdowns and some family members not talking to each other. You never expect that; you think it will pull people together. Having lost one of the strongest members of our family, a lot of the strength went with him. I feel like I have been tasked to fill his role, to the best of my ability, and that is what I will do. I will certainly ensure that the Wallen name is one associated with pride, dignity, respect, hard work, lover of the people and community, and always smiling. It is a firm name to be held up. I carry that baton right now; I will pass it on. This is the relay of life, you do your run, like he did when he passed the baton on to me. I will do my run and pass the baton on to Nathan no doubt, I wonder who he will pass the baton to?

I have to thank some of his best friends who have supported me in keeping his legacy alive. I am still in the dark period, but now I can see the light. Maybe that is the difference. The light that I can see is the motivation to make Sted proud.

My darkest days all happened within a 10-year block. I had such a good run before that, I had to get the bad patch, I had to feel lows to make me appreciate the good. The next stage of my life will be the best part of my life.

NOW I'M FAMOUS

Get around people who have something of value to share with you. Their impact will continue to have a significant effect on your life long after they have departed.

JIM ROHN

INFLUENCES

Mum

For most people, their mothers are their main influences. Mothers show you how you can go from nothing to something. We have always been something, so we went from not a lot to more. There are lessons to be found in watching how our mothers manage things. How they handle you and the whole family. How they stay on top of the multiple generations of kids and grandkids, keep the house clean, and go to work. We were never rich, but we were never hungry. We were never without shoes or clothes, and there are lots of people who have been far less fortunate than us and faced those difficulties. My mum has got to be my most significant influence, and even now as she is ageing, seeing her determination and strength makes me wonder how she does it. She still has her wits about her, she will still tell you about yourself and cuss you out if you've stepped wrong. She can still remember the plate you took 6 months ago, and she will not let it out of her memory until that exact plate is returned to the cupboard you found it in, she will remember where she got that plate 50 years ago and who she got the plate from. She is undoubtedly my biggest influence, growing up and to this day, and I think that will always be the case.

There have been quite a few key people who have been of influence in my life, and have contributed to my growth in some way, shape or form. They are all different types of people, of varying standing, but they have all contributed differently to helping me become the man that I am today.

In no particular order

Sted

Sted – my eldest brother, was a massive influence on me. He saw in me things that I never saw in myself. He saw something in me, and so from a very young age, he dedicated his time and efforts and decided that I was the brother he was going to focus on. He influenced me in how I do business, deal with people, my need for travel and meeting different people. I can gel in any room, with any audience, and with every type of person. I can firms the mans on road, and I can shake hands with Kings and Queens. I know how to adapt and fit in, and that is part of Sted's influence. He never gave up, he was forever pushing me and seeing him push himself, definitely influenced me. I remember there were times where he was doing day to day tasks for himself and made sure I saw it, and that would teach me without it being a direct lesson. He would tell me about his failures and mistakes, and they were lessons for me too. He paid the price for those mistakes so that I didn't have to repeat them later in life.

Even now, since he has passed, his teachings are still with me and resonate daily. He influenced my taste in everything; clothing, how I carry myself, appearance - as he was never shabby, approaching people, my taste in music, EVERYTHING. Sted introduced me to reggae as opposed to what was current at the time. My love of reggae comes from him. He came from Jamaica in the '70s and brought reggae to me. Without Sted I wouldn't be doing this book, firstly because I am doing it in memory of him, secondly because he always said he was going to write his own book, and didn't live long enough to get it done, so that influenced me to get shit done before it was too late. May, his great soul, rest in peace.

Sewa Singh Mandla

When I was studying law at college, I did my work placement at a company called Mandla and co. Solicitors, which was based on Soho Road, Handsworth Birmingham. It was founded by Mr Mandla himself, and he taught me so much about law, he gave me law books and took me to court with him during the week. He had me doing case files, he would sit behind me in court, and I would pass notes to him, and he to me, about what the person in the dock had just said. He taught me to update case files and prepare for the upcoming cases.

He asked me what I did on Saturdays, and I said "Not much, chilling with my friends, going up town", and he told me that my Saturdays could be better spent and asked me what I enjoyed doing. I told him I enjoyed chilling with my friends, but he asked me what else, and I told him that I enjoyed gardening. He then said that every Saturday morning I should go to his house and do his garden. Every Saturday morning! I was thinking maybe Saturday afternoon, or evening, as I was used to enjoying sleeping in on a Saturday, like most of my generation, but he said no, come at 9 am. I would get up, get ready and catch the bus to his house in Sandwell, it was a very long walk to his house down a lane, and it opened up into these big houses like I had never seen before. This man was well to do, and I thought – I would love to live like this one day, he drove a big black S class Mercedes too. He would pay me about a fiver to do his garden each Saturday. It wasn't a lot to do, I would cut the grass in the front and back gardens and pick some weeds – it was Mr Mandla who taught me how to cut the grass with the lines in, a skill that I am grateful for. Once I finished, he would invite me to his home to eat. His wife would prepare the food, he would sit in his chair, and I would sit on the floor to eat. He was a Sikh gentleman, he was very distinguished with a long white beard, he looked like he possessed a lot of wisdom. If you were to picture someone great, imparting wisdom – he looked the part. He would tell me stories, share words of knowledge, and gave me things to think about. He would ask me how my week was, not just work-related, and if I said I had argued with my brother, for example, he would advise me to go to my brother and say "I was wrong and you were wrong, and what is left? We are still brothers, let's put that behind us." It didn't matter what the scenario was, he always had a solution. For example, we had court one Monday morning, he asked me what time I was going to get to the office, and I said 9 am, as usual, he would say "this Monday, I am in at 8, come in at 8", and I thought to myself, why would I do that? 8 am was too early for me, but I did it, I got there at 8, and he asked me "What difference did coming in for 8 make to your day? Do you not feel fresher now than getting an hour's extra sleep, then jumping up and rushing to get here for 9, do you not feel better? Have a cup of tea and relax, read a book for the next 45 minutes". Reading was something you would never do in the mornings because you would get up and do what you need to do. He told me to get into the routine of getting up earlier, reading something and getting my mind in a certain place. This is something I have carried on doing, in particular with dropping my son Kayden off to school. I enjoy dropping him off because I like getting him set for the day. On the drive to school, we talk about anything and everything, but I get him motivated for school so that he isn't tired, and his brain is ticking in the morning. By the time he gets to the school gates, he is running in like he has been awake all day and he is motivated. Sometimes it is just making jokes for the entire journey. We pre-prepare ourselves to get ready to do what we need to do. Before I would just get ready to do it, like get up and get ready for work, but now I get up and read to prepare myself before getting ready for work. That has made a big difference to my life and that is something I have carried on from Mr. Mandla, a great gentleman, who has also, sadly, passed away. He was a massive influence in my life - even the fact that I chose to go to his house and do gardening, outdoors on a Saturday morning, says a lot about his influence. It wasn't a job that would bring me fame, fortune or kudos. It would have gotten me ridiculed by my friends for going to do some man's garden. The kudos would have come from going to town with my friends like I used to, chilling on the ramp in town and looking at girls - being the cool guy.

Sydney Bartley

Sydney Bartley came into my life when I was around 5 years old. He came to England not long after Sted did, to ensure Sted had settled in and had begun studying. During this time, he had also seen something in me. He was very strict, he was like the hated cousin, we loved him, but he gave you a headache. He was always on you, looking back now, it was so worth it, but at the time we would think "give me a break, I want to do my own thing". He was different to Sted, in that Sted was softer in his approach. Sted would tell you to do something, and he expected it of you, and if you didn't do it, he would say that the consequences are yours to hold, so be it. Sydney would sit there and made sure you were doing what he told you to. If he told you to read a book, he would say you are not moving until the book was finished and then he would ask you questions about it. I remember going out and saying I would be back at 8, by 1 minute passed 8, he would be at the window watching for me to come around the corner. If I were 5 minutes late, I would get the lecture "Don't you know about punctuality? If it was a train that you had to catch, could you turn up 5 minutes late? Would the train wait for you, no it wouldn't, would an aeroplane wait for you? No, it wouldn't, if you had to get to the bank to withdraw money, would the bank wait 5 minutes? No, so timing and punctuality are of the essence. Why wouldn't you use your head and say you are going to be here at 8.05 and be on time, rather than say 8 and be late? Or better yet, tell me 8.30 and exceed my expectations by getting here at 8.15?" he was adamant that you do what you say you are going to do. At the time he seemed to be a moaner, but he wasn't, he was just consistent and expected consistency. On another occasion, I was moving with the wrong crowd. We always had discussions about clothing, and we were a similar size, he used to like my shirts, so one day he went into my wardrobe to have a look at them, and he found a weapon. I remember coming home, and he was sat on my bed with his arms folded. He had it on the bed and was asking me about it. That night he lectured me until the early hours of the morning. He gave the type of lectures where your chest feels cold and your eyes water. He was giving me every scenario and making me understand the meaning of selfishness, how my actions and behaviours were selfish, how I was not thinking of the repercussions that they could have on anyone else, be it my mother, family, anyone else. From that day onwards, my life changed, it was an eye-opener. At that moment, I decided that that road was not for me and never would be. His guidance remains the same to this very day. He has mellowed slightly with age, and with me growing into the man I am today - thanks to his foundations, perhaps he feels his job is done. When I go to Jamaica, I feel proud that I can take him out and treat him. I tell him that I can do that because of the values he instilled in me. He is still solid and still one of my biggest mentors. I can call on him any time. There is never a period when I don't speak to him, and when I go to Jamaica, seeing him is always one of my priorities. If he is out of the country, we discuss timings, and he will try to fly back to see me. He is still a key influence now, someone that I can sit down and reason with. When I am doing my public speaking, I send him my stuff to look through and ask what he thinks of it, when I was doing my brother Steds funeral, I would send him stuff and ask his opinion. He is a man of stature, great wisdom, and understanding. If he is there for you, he will always be there for you. I am not the only person he has been there for; I have met some great people in Jamaica – members of parliament, bankers, lawyers, that he has been there for. He was a teacher originally, so he reached a lot of people. He gets a lot of perks too as they worship him, they all have stories about how he bought them their first schoolbook or their first shoes, this is what he does. If I can give back half of what he has, I'll be good. His legacy will live on, without a shadow of a doubt.

John Holcroft

John Holcroft, from Birmingham, was a big influence when I was up and coming. When I was starting a business, and I needed help from other local businesses, he was there for me. He was an outstanding Irish guy, and there were times when I needed help from my own community and they just weren't there - I had gone to them as my first point of call, I am a young black man, trying to do my own business and some of my own people didn't believe in me. John Alcroft was on a different level, he understood where I was coming from because he was a man in business and also a man from the streets. He gave me my second office for my charity BRO-SIS, I wanted to extend from my first office in Selly Oak, and I approached him saying that I already had staff, was running out of space, and I don't have the finances right now to expand. He said, in his strong Irish accent "don't worry about it, I will get you an office", and he did. That allowed me to run BRO-SIS Handsworth, which meant I could capture parts of the city that I wasn't able to reach in Selly Oak, another base for people to come to collect their condoms, get their checks done, and to get tested. To this day, he never charged me, he said we were to pay our phone bill and that it. He gave us a desk, a computer, and a phone, we just had to pay for our phone bill, but he didn't charge us rent. He gave us the key for the building and told us to keep it clean. He was straight up; he would say all of that in one day and leave, he wouldn't say come back and see me Thursday or Friday. He said if I wanted to show how serious I was about wanting the building, I was to start cleaning it out now, not tomorrow. When I began to work for BBC in London, he would have meetings in Birmingham with different local bodies, and he knew I loved him and would do things for him, so he would call me in the morning and say he had a meeting at 9am today and would ask me to go down and meet them. I would tell him I was in London, and he would say to me it was OK, that's only 2 hours away then would say "OK see you in 2 hours" and hang up before I could say anything else, so I would have to jump in my car or on a train and get back to Birmingham for his meetings. He was very black and white, there were no grey areas. He took over a new building in Villa Cross, it was completely empty, half of the building had no roof. He asked me what I thought he should do with the building as he was going to gut it. He told me to go away and think about it as the building was mine and gave me the keys. He told me "don't take the keys if you can't do something with it" and I turned the building into a local youth centre.

I wanted to use it as a sports hub, meeting hub, a creative hub, so I was designing where to put the toilets, and he gave me free rein to do so. All he did was come and see how I was getting on and from time to time, asked me what I needed, I'd say I needed a plumber, and he would give me a number and tell me to say he had sent me. He paid for it all, he would buy the toilets and tell me the plumber will be there on Wednesday, I would meet them and show them where to put them. He was very much like Sted in that way. He has also passed away. He was a very good man, he also helped my good friends Errol Lawson, and Nathan Dennis. We all came away from that experience with the mindset to help the community.

Gregory Isaacs

Gregory Isaacs, the Reggae artist, The icon, Mr Cool himself, The Cool Ruler, The ladies man...do you see the comparison already? Gregory was also a massive influence; some people say I am starting to look like him now. Sted introduced me to the music of Gregory Isaacs in the 70s, he was known as the cool ruler and always looked the part. He always looked sharp, which was different from all the other Reggae artists - he always wore a hat and suit. He dressed like an English man, 3-piece suit, ties, or bowler hats. He was always pristine - that was a massive influence. The other influence came from the fact that his songs were always about love and peace, he was also a lady's man, that rubbed off on me. I was certainly that man in the past. Sted allowed me to meet him once. That was a dream come true for me. I then pursued him and kind of stalked him for the rest of my life. There were several occasions where I had found out where he was, and I would get connected to people around him so that I could get to him. I got to the point where I used to chat with his daughter, and we became good friends. I still go and look at his house off Red Hills Road when I'm in Jamaica, it has a blue plaque on it now to show he lived there. It's about 3 minutes from my house, so I pass by there. It wasn't until it had the blue plaque that I realised that that was where he lived. Someone had shown me a different house as his, but I knew where his studio and shop were, and I used to go there also. He had a record shop called African Museum record shop, and the studio was African Museum Studios, where he produced a lot of his own songs. He was one of the first independent producers that created their own music. He also influenced me as many people in the world know of his struggles in life and the issues he had with beating drugs, but he always came out on top. It did not stop him, the drugs and the arrests didn't stop him. He never gave up. Apparently, he had been arrested or went to jail over 50 times for various charges. He went to prison on gun and drug charges, and still came out and was the man that could pull crowds of 10,000+ in brazil. Through all his problems and everything else, I loved his perseverance. Also, it is documented that he had 10 children and raised all 10. He took all 10 to live in his house, with his wife, who had no children of her own. She said he would come home from tour, and before he locked the door, he would go in each room and count them to make sure they were there. He had a deal with all of their mothers that he was taking his children to live with him. That speaks to me as a father. Having been able to be in his presence, being in the same room or at shows with him. That man has a presence when he walks into a room, I'm not sure if it is because I am a super fan, but others have agreed, he has such a presence. When some people enter a room, they just enter a room, but when he entered, even without saying a word, you knew he was there. He had this walk that I will never forget, his shoulders were back, it was humbling but powerful. Once he did a show in Digbeth, and after the show, he came into the VIP room, casually, almost in slow motion, and hail at everybody. You could hear a pin drop. Then he would say "I'm not going to eat all of this, nor am I going to drink all of this" referring to all of the food, liquor and champagne, "Don't make anything go to waste, grab a bottle" even that was different. At the hummingbird, down a long corridor, he was in his changing room, and everyone was outside waiting to get autographs, and he just walks out onto the landing in his string vest, shirt open, gold chain, hat cotched off, big spliff, and greets everyone "everybody good?" he always spoke in Rasta tongues. If someone asked for a picture and he couldn't do it right then, he would make sure to come back to them, telling them not to move and to wait. Another time he had finished a show, but the crowd wanted more, he had finished, but the crowd was still there chanting his name, at this time I am standing by the stage door. I saw him walking through the crowd and leave through the arena exit. I followed his crew and asked him to sign a picture, he stopped and agreed. Then he said "matter of fact, I am keeping it, I like this picture of myself" and walked off with my picture. So now, I have a felt hat, and as I am ageing, I don't have his locks, but I can sing like him, I reckon I can do a mad Gregory tribute. Sted always asked me to sing like him, at every opportunity. No other artist has influenced me like Gregory Isaacs has, it's through his music, his style, personality, his drive, determination, family values and overcoming his struggles that drew me to the person outside of the music.

Bounty Killer

Bounty Killer has also had an influence on me, and that's because he has always been a defender of the poor, helping others, supporting them and bringing through as many people as he could, that is a measure of success too, not just what you achieve, but who you bring through.

Raj Bagri

Raj Bagri is a good friend of mine, and he may not realise that he has been an influence on me. He has helped me understand humbleness, to a different level. We go back years, we worked together. He also showed me true loyalty; he is one of few friends I have had from day one. We have never had bad words or any issues, even if we don't speak for 6 months, that message or call will come through. People don't have to be in your immediate circle to be relevant, so long as they remain in your heart, that's what matters. When Sted passed, I knew he was there. He is also a very hard worker, he showed me a good strong work ethic and a very good hustling ethic. Raj also influenced me to stay clear of alcohol lol, at a work do I got disgustingly drunk, Raj kindly ensured I reached home safe and took me to my mums in a taxi, as she opened the door, I think I threw up in my cousins hand. It was the worst feeling ever, Raj reminded me of my drunken behaviour and since then some 30 years on I've never been drunk again. My mum still speaks of that event and always praises Raj for getting me home safely and because of these things, I will say he has been one of my influences.

Avtar Obhi

Another good friend of mine called Avtar Obhi has influenced me because he is the most peaceful and humble brother that I know. Calming, peaceful and humble. If he had £10 million, it wouldn't make any difference in him sharing his food with you, if he had £20 million, it wouldn't change him saying "your lace is undone, I will tie it for you" he is the humblest man, calm like no one's business, he is so at peace with the world, and with life, it makes you want to be in his presence. No matter what you are going through, he will give you a settling feeling and make you realise what is truly important or give you an understanding as to why it is OK to feel upset. He is not deeply religious to the point that he will push it in your face, but he is able to extract some things from his faith as a Sikh man, that can help you.

Aunt Claire

My Aunt Claire has been a big influence since I was a child, she has been there for me through every bit of my journey, through my dancing days, through my bad days, and now she has influenced me to go to church; she hasn't forced me to become a Christian, but she has allowed me to see that there is a bigger force behind all that is happening around me. Now I'm famous along with my stylist, PA and security, my Aunt Claire will certainly be part of my entourage as my spiritual advisor.

Helen Platt

In my latter years, a lady that I met while at the BBC called Helen Platt. She always believed in me, even at times when I doubted myself and thought a task was too big, she would always say "nope you can do it, apply yourself and you can do it, I wouldn't put it to you if I didn't believe you could do it" she acted as my agent, in terms as different projects, locally and nationally. When I thought the spec was too much for me, she would tell me I was capable. When the projects were very large, and I would need to get a team in, she would say to me that I could do it either on my own or with a team. She always made me feel capable of mastering any project or contract that was thrown at me. To this day, nothing that she has given me, have I failed on. They are part of my success stories, and I have to give credit to Helen Platt as an influencer. Helen, Yusef and myself were the founders of Somewhereto, and they brought me in in the early stages, it was Helen that believed I could help shape it and together we made it what it is today. Unilever, Shift, many major companies, and contracts have come to me through Helen. When she would bring a massive project and I would say it's too big, or it would take 6 months, she would say "come on, you can do it" or "sort out managing your time better" Helen knew one of my weak points was that I hated paperwork, I am practical, I do the stuff, but I hated the paperwork. It was Helen that helped me find the balance with doing the paperwork to show the work I had put in and document the 100 people we helped, for example. She even built a spreadsheet for me, to make my life easier to document, she gave me a template to fill in on my iPad to fill in each night and send off to show what I had done. She even added a field for me to put in pictures of the day, of the people that I had met and helped. Helen also helped me to become an excellent bid writer in terms of adapting previous bids to match the new one. Study the funder first, find out what they want to fund, and make sure your project matches their goals. Back in the day, I would focus on what I wanted to achieve but now I know to better align them. I didn't realise she was such a big influencer until I started talking about her. She works with a guy Finn Tayler who is a professional photographer, he has worked for some massive companies and huge celebrities. Still, he says that some of his best work that he has done has been with me, on the ground, getting into the gritty photos of incredible people, that aren't famous or popular, but incredible characters. He can capture personalities through his lens, you can look into the people's eyes and see their personality. His pictures tell a thousand words. I am influenced by his concepts of looking deeper into most things. I now look beyond the photo, and he explains it so well.

God

I am not religious, but I am probably more in touch with religion now than I have ever been, I have been going to church, praying more often and reading the Bible occasionally. I believe in prayer, I believe in the unseen God, a stronger force than me, that is making everything happen. Since I have been in that place, I don't know if it is mind over matter, but I feel that my life is alright. Whether it is him or not, I don't know, but it's working.

Shelika

My daughter, Shelika, is a fighter. When she battled and won the fight against Cancer in 2007-2008, she spent 13 months in Sheffield Hospitals in a Teenage Cancer unit, I used to travel there and sleep in the room with her. Sometimes I felt useless, and it felt surreal other times, I was scared that the Cancer would spread and that I'd lose her, but her spirit always made me know I still had her. Shalika had a way that by looking at me, I just knew she was saying "Dad everything's going to be OK". With her spirit, I could rock any illness. She has been my influence to get through anything when you are hit with Cancer, and it has the stigma related to death, she lost all her hair, but she never lost her spirit. She said "Dad, come and help me choose a wig" and she would wear bandanas in hospital. A talking point for Shelika and me was that some of the wigs she chose were proper shite. Not even the most hardened shoplifter would steal that from Beauty Queens. She had her down days, but she had days when you would not think that she was going through chemotherapy. She has that spirit, laughter, and jokes all the time. She was still in treatment when we threw her 18th birthday party at my house, she still had her tubes in from chemotherapy, but it didn't stop her from partying hard. That drive and the refusal to be beaten or stopped. She got that determination from me. I have influenced her, and she has influenced me. Now watching her grow into a young, beautiful, successful businesswoman, and a mother too. When you are that close to death, and you come through and own your own shit, your own car, your own property, in a good job, earning more now than I was at her age, she should be very proud. She is doing so well; she is very confident and a new mum. To have been in a faraway hospital for over a year, it's a long time, and to be far away from family too, and to come through like she did, it inspires me. She fought that fight and won. Watching her through that journey has taught me, like everything else, that this too shall pass.

AN AUTOBIOGRAPHY BY TERENCE WALLEN

> *"The world is a book, and those who do not travel read only one page."*
> **SAINT AUGUSTINE**

AN AUTOBIOGRAPHY BY TERENCE WALLEN

TRAVELLING

Travelling is an integral part of my growth, and it really should be part of everyone's growth. When we a born, we are raised in a bubble. As a youngster, my parents couldn't afford to take me on a plane, we didn't have any trips to Europe in the 6-week holidays like young people have now. All of my 6 weeks holidays, throughout school, were pretty much spent at home, summer school and playing out. However, I never felt like I was missing out. My first plane trip was back in 1991 to Germany. Our cousin Sydney was the director in the ministry of culture, he was touring and doing his thing on behalf of Jamaica. He was a guest speaker and invited me to go with him to Germany. We stayed at a friend of his called Henner Bloomer. It really opened my eyes to how big the world is. All of a sudden, it seemed huge. You would look at the globe and wonder if you could ever travel to the countries and places you see there. Now it is much easier, but then it felt so big. I experienced a new language in Germany, met new people, saw how other people lived and ate. It was such an eye-opener. Since then, I have never stopped travelling. I have some main countries that I visit again and again. I go to Europe often, as over the years I made new friends and created new networks. In my time travelling, some of the key places that have influenced me as a person were Germany, as that made me see how big the world was, how easy it was to travel and the fact that I had a passport that is like a ticket to anywhere as well as the following:

Jamaica

The first time I went to Jamaica was in 1993, I went as the guest of a government official – which was my cousin Sydney. I had the diplomat, international visitor treatment. I wasn't like a typical English youth landing there, I was met on the tarmac, he was waved through customs, everyone was shaking his hands. I was blown away and felt so proud. When everyone else was queuing, I was in the VIP section. I felt like I had arrived, when we stepped outside, there was a stretch Mercedes with people opening the doors for us to go in. I remember thinking that I could get a taste for this life. Maybe that shaped what I wanted from life, being surrounded by people like Sydney, at such a young age, it gave aspirations and a taste for that lifestyle.

Jamaica was a massive eye-opener for me, it felt like I was going home. I visited my mum's house, my dad's house, I saw where they were born, and it was a history lesson for me. I had never met any of my grandparents, visiting and seeing their graves in the garden, that was a poignant moment. When I saw the house that my mother grew up in, it's not much bigger than my office now, but coming from that small place, made me think, "look at what my mother has achieved". I loved every minute of being in Jamaica, it was like paradise. It is probably my most visited country as I am totally in love with it, and every visit I still feel like it is paradise and heaven, I think the vibe of love there and it's like the first time. I still have family in Jamaica, great friends, and some great business opportunities. Being there also gives you a deeper understanding of the culture of Jamaicans. It gave me a better appreciation of the way that they were raised, their schooling, upbringing, and how they lived. I have learned so much. The food and fresh fruit are out of this world. All these things that were brand new to my way of thinking.

My complete love of everything Jamaican and Jamaica itself as a country is real. Though sometimes its portrayal isn't the best, as with every country in the world, it has its negatives, but the vibe there is second to none, just the smell of Jamaica has a power. It has a good feeling from the moment you land. The heat, the people, the vibe, you hear music everywhere you go. Music plays such a big part in Jamaica, it is the only place I know where there is a party every single night of the week, and every single day without fail, you will hear music on the street. There is always an energy on the street, even if you are not going anywhere in particular, you can get just as much vibe from chilling on the corner as you would at a party. I absolutely love Jamaica. There are places like Montego Bay and Ocho

Rios, which are very lovely, and touristy; however, I spend a lot of my time in Kingston, as that's where I feel the real vibes. If you haven't been to Kingston, I don't really feel like you have been to Jamaica, you can stay in a hotel in the tourist areas and think "wow, this is the Caribbean, its beautiful", but you won't know Jamaica until you get outside the hotel walls and go into the inner city. People say it is dangerous, and it is, you have to be somewhere connected and have links to stay safe, but I go down there, and I speak patois, do my thing, sometimes it fits in, sometimes it doesn't, and it sounds stupid. I love Trench town, Jones town, Allman town, I love Callaloo bay, opposite Riverton, that's where Bounty Killa comes from, amongst others. That's ghetto and where most of the crime takes place, but if you are in it and a part of it, it is probably where you would feel the safest. The vibe there is heavenly. Many times, I have given up staying in the big house in Red Hills, Beverly hills or Cherry gardens just to be down in the ghetto, so you can have that long vibe. Clarendon is where my parents came from, it's a lovely place and its country, so there are a lot of open cane fields. It doesn't have the same energy as the town, which is hustle and bustle, you can get everything and barter. Kingston is my number 1 place; I keep returning there. I have reached the point that when I am going to Jamaica, I feel like I am going home. I have a home in Jamaica now, as I am there so often it made sense to have one. It has its downsides, you have to be on top of your shit, as you can blink and lose it all. It can be very hard and corrupt. Money runs Jamaica, you have to have your wits about you there. You can't be absent-minded or timid as they are very smart and money can get you more or less, any and everything done in Jamaica.

When you think about all of the greats that come out of that very small country, you have to understand that it is a very blessed place. To be the womb of reggae music, which is worldwide. The home of the fastest man in the world. The home of one of the most famous artists in the world, Bob Marley. The best Ganja in the world. All of this is from a tiny island. Millions of tourists go there every single year, wanting to experience the beauty of this place. I recommend everyone at some point must go and visit Jamaica.

AFRICA

Workwise, I have travelled a fair bit. I love Africa, I have worked there quite a lot and have been to Kenya, Malawi, Namibia, and Zimbabwe. I have done a trek in the Sahara Desert, Algeria, Libya, and Egypt. That was my first feel of that side of Africa, which is entirely different from the other parts I had visited. The Sahara trek was very humbling as it was quite primitive. I was used to travelling in luxury, but the hotels for the trek were very old fashioned if you get one channel on the TV, which was downstairs in the hallway, you were lucky. They had English newspapers such as The Sun and Telegraph that was 2 or 3 weeks old.

I had already read them back home before I came to Africa and had thrown them out. Sleeping on the beds was like sleeping on rocks. It was an incredible experience to see how other people live. I went to Namibia to speak at a conference on HIV/AIDs. Kenya had a bit of a party vibe, though I was working, we enjoyed ourselves. Malawi, I think, had the most profound effect on me. I went there to deliver a project for the BBC, and it was during this time working out there, that I felt like I had gone home, to a whole new family. The people of Malawi treat you like a king, they were so beautiful. There were a lot of deserts, mud huts and water points instead of running water in their village. It was the most beautiful place I have been to in Africa. I was working in HIV and AIDs and to see people out there living with HIV/AIDs, there is a different look to them there to those living with HIV/AIDS here in the UK. Seeing everything firsthand in Malawi, changed my life. It humbled me, I wanted to be there, and I am still in touch with a few key people that I met there.

Hong Kong

I worked in Hong Kong as an international sales and marketing manager for a big watch company. My role was to help get the watches out around the world. Some parts of the watches were made in Hong Kong, so I had to fly out to oversee the design and manufacturing of those parts. I could not eat much of the food in Hong Kong; everything is alive until you want it cooked, and that put me off totally. When you go to the market, all of the ingredients are moving. You're going to buy food, but it feels like you're walking into a zoo. That put me off. One word of warning for Hong Kong – be careful of the women/men. One minute you are talking to this beautiful Asian queen, the next minute you are staring into an Adam's apple lol. The people of Hong Kong work very hard, and the fashion is really good there. Also, there is an excellent mixture of people there, a lot of east and west Asian, Africans too. It was very packed and busy.

America

I used to travel to America a lot too. Mainly Florida, as my dad lived there for 14 or 15 years, so I went to see him, and in the night go out and party in Miami. As I was going to Jamaica quite often, it was just a short hop over to Miami and back again. I loved Florida; it has outstanding energy about the place. Fort Lauderdale is like a mini Jamaica but with a little more money. I visited New York, and California in America too, but I think Florida was my favourite place to go to in America.

Being British

Being British, we have the ability to travel all around the world, with minimal struggle. Whereas people from other countries, would struggle to come here, so I like to utilise the fact that I am British born and bred to travel, to go out and meet new people and learn new things. I remember in Kenya was the first time I decided to try different types of meat, such as buffalo, crocodile, alligator, and even zebra. What is repulsive to us is often a delicacy in other parts of the world.

If you're thinking about going travelling, just get on a plane and go. Travelling is a huge part of my life; I don't think there has been a year that I haven't travelled. It helps my sanity; it gets me away from the hustle and bustle of life here. It gets me away from work, the kids, family, it is my downtime, and everyone deserves to be able to take a break and be in a different place. As I get older, I realise how small the world is and how accessible everywhere is. Some places felt impossible to get to when I was younger, like Australia, I used to think there was no way to get there, but now, if you are willing to take the long flights, you can go anywhere.

When I was younger, I also did the partying, I visited Ibiza and Malia. I don't have any regrets, but looking back, visiting those places did not have any impact on me at all, but the others I have mentioned made a real difference to me.

I would recommend and encourage anyone, young and old, to get some travelling under your belt. Even if you live in England and it is just to travel to Wales, come out of your zone and community, see other parts of the world. Meet new people and broaden your horizons and thinking. Broaden your portfolio while you are at it, make use of the new networks and new ideas' available everywhere. You never know when the new contacts that you make will come in handy, and you can utilise them down the road.

"Rich people have small TVs and big libraries, and poor people have small libraries and big TVs."
ZIG ZIGLAR

AN AUTOBIOGRAPHY BY TERENCE WALLEN

ACCUMULATION OF WEALTH

Money brings independence and certain levels of freedom. I left home when I was 16 as I wanted independence, and never looked back. I have always said that "I will never return to my mother's house, I will get a big enough house for her to come and live with me". I rented a flat in a high-rise block, the main entrance stank of piss, but once you walked into my flat, on the fourth floor, it was NICE. It was a nice flat for where it was, I was the only one in the whole block with leaded windows – which I did myself. I had a green carpet, green leather sofas, and a fish tank, and I knew it was a nice, clean pad. I could not play chess, but I had a glass chess table. I was always working, so that allowed me the finances to have that freedom and enjoy those luxuries from 16. I lived comfortably, and that showed in my image, which meant that I attracted people of similar standing. I moved into an apartment in a more affluent area – Hamstead. It was peaceful, and the neighbours were lovely. It was a small development with only 8 apartments. I had a Saab with black leather interiors, and then an MG convertible.

I was able to move up, and you have to be financially savvy to be able to have that growth at such a young age. If you can't afford the growth, you should be in a position where you are working towards growing and building. I have never been a fan of credit. I don't believe in getting something now and paying later, as you will often have to pay more if you do that. I had to build my credit profile to get a mortgage, but I have never been one to use credit to live. I much prefer to save and then get what I want. I don't spend excessively on things that don't add value or real joy to my life. I like watches, so I spend money on watches, I would probably spend more on a watch than I would on a car. I do drive nice cars, but they aren't a passion of mine. I like to have a nice home, so I spend money on my houses. I don't smoke, do drugs or spend weekends partying as that just burns money. The concept of smoking, of spending money on something and setting it alight seems like a waste to me. I like to see and feel what I have spent my money on, I like to get use out of it. I can rock a £20 Diesel t-shirt and a 50k watch because I am a lover of watches, and I am not overly interested in designer clothes.

I have always been good with money, I bought the house I am living in now, at a good time. I bought it during the recession and got it at a good price. I invested in bricks. The watches that I bought back then have held their value well too. If shit hit the fan, I could sell them too. I invested wisely in the past, and that has allowed me to live comfortably now. I have always landed good jobs, and I have always known my worth, in terms of working smarter instead of harder, and knowing what I would get out of bed for. That applies to my freelance contracting work too, for companies like the BBC that needed my services around youth development or social impact. My rate is my rate, take it or leave it, I know my worth. Fortunately for me, I had built a solid reputation around the quality of the work that I delivered, which meant I could set a good price and companies would not bat an eyelid in paying it. I had references from massive companies that said that I was the right man for the job, and if they wanted the job to be done correctly, then they would have to pay for it. I started at a young age with roles at £3 an hour and moved to roles that pay £200 or £300 an hour. Once you understand your worth, and others do too, they will pay it. Though money is a good driver, it is not my sole driver. I find that if you meet the needs of other things, like doing good and helping people, then money will come. Now if the money doesn't come, your financial needs will be met in another way. I have had a lot of "in-kind" support because of things I have done for others in the past that have helped people make, or save, a lot of money, so when the times comes around, if they are not paying me financially, they allow me to get a service in kind, which has value too. I have been fortunate to have a lot of services and products that I have not had to pay for, because of who I was and who I helped in the past. I have put on events and saved thousands by making phone calls and have had people provide it for free. I have had PA equipment supplied for free by DJ's that remember when I didn't take my cut of their pay packet for a set, and it wasn't much money, but they remember it. I am still able to save a lot of money and live comfortably because of what I used to do. People always give back and show gratitude, for when I showed sincerity and supported them at a time when they needed it.

Saving has helped me to not have to work so hard today and have some passive income streams. I have leases on properties that people rent. I often refuse freelance contracts simply because I don't want to work for a few months, as the value that I place on life now isn't about making money, it is about making the time to spend with my mum or my children. My priorities have changed now, money was a priority in the early days, but that has allowed me the time and space to enjoy my family now. There is a saying "Entrepreneurship is about living a few years of my life like most people won't so that I can live the rest of my life like most people can't."

It isn't about what I can give to my kids or grandkids financially, it's about what lessons I can instil in them and what legacy I can leave. The children will be able to go out and earn their own money, they will not always depend on you to keep them going. What they will need from you is to set the foundations and the morals that will allow them to be successful. If you throw money at them, that is dead money, but lessons will carry them.

I haven't always been successful in every business. I have put on events that lost money and lent out money that hasn't come back. I invested early in cryptocurrency, and many others weren't doing that, and it still hasn't reached its peak, but who is to say if that will come to fruition in the next ten years? That is what life is like, sometimes you have to take those risks, it's like gambling. I don't go out and gamble on the horses, this is my risk. Life is about risk and investing, you have to put it in to get it back out. Do not let the fear of the risk stop you from going for it. If I lose £10k now, I then look at ways to make £10k back. I have had people or business partners what I have invested in and lost, but it always came to an end when I wasn't meant to lose any more. If I had lost £1million, then that was my threshold, if I hadn't lost that, if something hadn't intervened and meant I lost that much, then I could have carried on investing and I could have lost £2million. I have invested in people for years and then found out that they were unscrupulous. If I hadn't found out then, I could have carried on supporting and investing in them for longer, thinking they had a clean heart. Yes, I may have lost £1million, but I could have carried on and lost £2million or £3million, so I have been saved. That then drives me to go and make my £1million back. I have the knowledge and experience to make it again. I know I will never be hungry or homeless, even if I can't afford these things, I know someone will support me because of what I have done previously. I know I have the skills to go out and make that money back. I have faith in myself to be able to make back any losses.

Money is not as important as people think it is. There are many people nowadays that are more interested in looking successful than being actually successful, which is backwards to me. People portray wealth and riches, but don't have it, because they are more concerned about others perceptions of them than being realistic about their current circumstances. In order to be successful, you have to work hard. Unless you are lucky enough to win the lottery or inherit a couple million, you must work hard. A lot of people don't want to work hard at any point. You can put in 5 years of hard graft and rest for the next 5, but you have to put that work in. I feel like I have been putting that work in for a long time. Now I work a 4- or 5-hour day, of an evening. I used to work 12-hour days and had no social life, but that got me to where I am now. My days are mine now, I can spend time with my mum, my children, and my grandson. It also frees me up to be able to give back to the community in regard to my consulting. Some of my consulting, I do charge for, but sometimes it comes naturally, and I share my experiences and knowledge. A lot of the knowledge that I have, I got for free, so I can share that for free. Some of my expertise, depending on who needs it, costs money to get access to. I will always have time for people, I still want to give back. Many people continue to lean on me for help, advice and support, and when I look at people that I have helped, who have become successful, that is where I see my success. I don't ask for a return or a percentage of their success, all I want is to know that they have made it, they have achieved their goals and are doing well.

If you asked me if I am successful - yes, Am I a millionaire? Does it matter if I am or I'm not? Have I peaked? No, once the people that I have helped and influenced reach their peak, that is when I reach mine.

"I make a living by what I get, but I make a life by what I give"

#**MYTRUTH**

GIVING BACK

Giving back is just as crucial as acquiring assets and wealth. Giving back should always be part of everyone's journey. It doesn't matter what, or how much you give back, but you should give back.

I have given back in different ways. One of these ways is time, and time is valuable. People don't put a financial value on time, but if I can work for £200 an hour, and I choose to give you an hour for free, my in-kind gesture is worth £200. The other value is that I could have been doing something of great importance to me, which means you have to value my time. When I give back, people appreciate that I am giving them my time and expertise. It has cost me a lot of time and money, over the years to have gained this knowledge and wisdom, that I am now passing onto someone else, in the hope that they can run with it and use that knowledge to make something good of themselves. You have to value what it cost me to get to that point. That comes from a greater understanding of your self-worth. I have given back by mentoring a lot of people. Guiding them and being there for them, be that in person, on the phone or via email. It could be as simple as a WhatsApp message in the morning saying "I hope you kickstart your day well and remain focussed" which can help start their day well. I have mentored some people who have gone on to become very successful, and they never forget that. Some are successful in music, some in sport, and others in business.

Giving back should be in everybody's journey just as corporate responsibility is a part of business now.

I have also given back by employing people. Any time I have set up a business, an event or company, I have made sure that I can have a workforce that I can tap into and employ people. I took that approach from very early on, in Supremes nightclub, Brosis, Birmingham Sports and Culture day - that has been running for 21 years, I have always employed my own people. I am giving people the opportunity to earn and learn at the same time. I have been bringing people through with me, sometimes they started as volunteers, but they gained valuable experience and built their network. I invite my people to join me at black-tie events, which gets them into a room with a combined value of £50million, where they might have been in a room with a combined value of £20. They can then network in that black-tie event and walk out with connections that take them closer to becoming a millionaire. So many big deals are started not just in a boardroom, they are made through a social acquaintance. Coffee houses and dinner dances have been the home to many conversations that led to big deals. The papers may have been signed in a board room, but the initial discussions were in a social setting. Sometimes I will go to an event that is £150 per head, and I may bring 10 young people to sit around the table with me, the value isn't in the fact that I have paid for a 4 course meal, it is in the fact you are now in the correct setting and surrounded by people of power and influence. Putting people in those spaces is part of my giving back.

Another way that I give back is by recommending people from within my network, to others. I often suggest people that I know have the skills for a required project. I don't take a cut of the deal, I never ask for a monetary reward for putting people in line for work, I don't act as a middleman and take 5% of what they make from the deal. If they choose to buy me a ginger beer to say thanks, I won't say no, but it isn't my motivation - It is part of my giving back.

My charity and humanitarian work – you reach a stage where giving back becomes natural. Some people think if you rise out of the hood, that you have to carry everyone from the community with you, the reality is that you don't have to do that. Marcus Garvey once said "I have no desire to take all black people back to Africa, there are blacks here that are no good here, and likewise, would be no good there" and that concept says to me, that when you grow up in an inner-city area, don't feel like you have to take everybody with you. Some people that are no good in the inner city will be no good up there either. What you have to do is take the best of your inner circle with you, as they will be good wherever you put them, and with that, they will then also influence others. That is my philosophy when giving back. That itself has its downsides, some people may think I am from the ends, but I don't give back. It's not about going around on an open-back truck, throwing out chickens at Christmas, or handing out wads of money to everyone. I would rather make it big, invest my time and effort into individuals who will also make it big, and they will then take that attitude forward and help others as I helped them. To me, that works better than handouts. I give back to lots of people, who will then give back to lots of people - the cycle will continue, and my legacy will remain. I don't want to be remembered because I gave out 50 chickens on Christmas eve, I don't want to be known as the chicken man. I want to be known as the man with a legacy of changing people's lives for the better. You have to know how, and when to give back. There will be times when you are not ready to give back, and you should not be pressured to do so just because the rest of the world thinks that you must be ready. You decide when you are ready.

Here in the UK and abroad I still do a lot of charity work. I have personally sponsored several establishments in Jamaica, including a primary inner-city school, Callaloo Mews, which is off the Spanish Town Rd in Kingston. It is a very deprived community, it is barely touched by the government out there, it's as though they barely recognise that they still exist. I still visit that school when I am out there. I sponsored the Allman Town Police Youth Club, one of the great leaders there is Mr

Kevin Walker, who is a very dear friend of mine. I love his passion and drive to bring about change in that inner-city area that battles crime, drugs and violence, and in the midst of it all, he is seeking out young people and supporting them through this youth club. They meet regularly, host events and organise trips for them. For them to have a place of peace, in an area like that, is a big achievement, and I have been supporting the youth club for years. I take part in their workshops, I support them financially as well as offering advice and support, I send them things over from the UK too, like free condoms, for example.

I support and visit Trout Hall All-Age School in Clarendon, which is where my parents are from. I got involved through a good friend of mine, who I had mentored and supported here in the UK. He went onto greater things and had moved to Antigua, working in a fantastic organisation and helped up a team that supports the schools that they had been to. There is a school called Tower hill Basics, which I helped to buy their classroom equipment, such as chairs and tables. In St Mary there is a school called Smart Start learning centre, I supported them and bought computers, printers and DVD players to help them achieve their dreams and the aspirations of the young kids who want to become great individuals and great leaders. They are inner-city schools that I knew would benefit from my help. £500 won't go very far here in the UK, but in Jamaica, it can buy the tables and chairs for a classroom, and books that last for a year or two. I don't go into the inner-city areas and buy cars, I like to invest in the long term, and the education and support of the young people. I also give back so much here in the UK too. I help, support, guide and mentor many people. I still volunteer my time with some organisations that call upon me for things like public speaking, youth workshops or even painting a community centre wall. You can call on me to give back as that's what I am about. People see the value in that, I think that is why people don't beg me for financial support, they can see that I am already doing my fair share. I think there would be more pressure if people thought I wasn't doing anything for the community.

The weight of mentoring is heavyweight. You always have to deal with other people's lives and their lifestyles. Although you genuinely have an interest in their wellbeing and want them to do well in life. You can sometimes have an uphill battle with the other influences in their life. Just like our parents, you sometimes have to hope that you have instilled enough inside them, that will resonate inside their heads. So that when you're not with them, they will be able to analyse right from wrong, or even if the wrong idea outweighs the good, at least they had a choice and made a conscious decision. It is essential to be consistent. I must always remain that person. As a mentor, I have to see myself as a Shepard and be consistent in my outgoings, verbally and physically. I have to continually work on myself. Being consistent is hard. If I say I'm a mentor, I mean, I am there until one of us passes away, but my words will always be there. Passing the baton on is a part of mentoring, so hopefully, if I do enough for a mentee, then that mentee can add value to someone else, in an entirely new capacity.

The community will always be important to me. Community isn't just where I came from, in terms of the immediate area. It is very much about the makeup of the area and the people in it. If it were just the geographical area, I wouldn't support those that had moved out of it. It is about the people that come from that community. I have moved out of the area that I am from, but I am very much rooted and have a standing in the community there, as did Sted. He had moved out of the area, but he was still a man of standing in Handsworth. I am incredibly proud of the fact that I am from Handsworth, and I will always give back to them and the surrounding areas. The more people that buy this book is the more that I can give back.

ACKNOWLEDGMENTS

Acknowledgment of all the people's contributions to the achievement of my goals can be one of the most valuable attitudes I'll ever cultivate.

You need to know the role of luck, circumstances, and success will never go to my head - and that's the only way to preserve it.

First and foremost, I would like to thank The Almighty. In the process of putting this book together, I realized how true this gift of writing is for me. You have given me the power to believe in my passion and pursue another of my dreams. I could never have done this without the faith I have in you, the Almighty.

To my mother, Gloria Wallen: For the first time in years, I am speechless! I can barely find the words to express all the wisdom, love and support you've given me. You are my #1 fan and for that, I am eternally grateful. If I am blessed to live long enough, I hope I will be as good a father to my children as you are and always have been a mother to me. I Love You Mommy x

Ps. I promise to bring back your plate lol

To my ride or die Nathan aka Nates/CEO: What can I say? You are one of the main reasons that it makes sense! I am so thankful that I have you in my corner pushing me when I am ready to give up. All the good that comes from this book and future publications (3 book half million deal lol) I look forward to sharing with you! You are my nephew, my brother and my best friend. Thanks for not just believing, trusting the journey, standing firm in the storm, but knowing that I could do this and that my loyalty would eventually reward us both. I Love You Always & Forever!

To my Sons & Daughters: You are the best thing that I have ever done in my life! You welcomed me into Fatherhood and I am so grateful for you. You are the ones in this world I would give my life for. You gave me something to work for. A better life for you than I had is all I wanted. Dad loves you more than you will ever know and my drive to make a change is because of you.

Shelika....what a journey, you're an inspiration, your own fight for life, your love of life, Child...you've held me together from day one, never failing me even when id fail you, how can you be so much like me? it's scary, you actually make me laugh every single time we communicate, now you have blessed me with my 1st Grandchild, what more can I ask for...Glam-Dad Tezza at the controls!!! One thing I'm yet to master is how you still manage to get money out of me when you a big rartid woman lol, I'll say it now so its documented, keep Shelika away from my wheelchair if I ever end up in one, cos she will see the funny side of pushing me down hills in the snow lol

My Tribe....every father deserves to get the love I do, you kids make it all worth it, and I hope the foundations I've instilled in you have set you up for a life of greatness, knowledge & understanding.

Jamel...your solid, always have been and always will be. Keep on keeping on, your love of family is inspiring. I'm so proud of you, stand firm, the world is at your fingertips. We won't always see eye to eye, but we'll always see heart to heart 🧡.

Keyon...I'm so proud of you too, consistent in your progress, your personality, your attitude to life and making the best of all opportunities is an inspiration to me and others. From the shy daddy's boy to the infamous Instagram videos lol, I love it!! Well done Shabba!🧡.

Téja - Daddy's princess, always the perfect child, your smile warms every situation, I'm so proud of you, continue to embrace your empress status, the world is your oyster, beautiful inside & out, forever my Teeeejah 🧡.

Kayden - Daddy's boy, you have made the last 6 years of my life one of going from strength to strength. Your loving nature holds me, your comical personality, your constant hugs & kisses grips my every being. I'm so proud of you, keep on showing that loving side and watch how the world falls at your feet 🩷.

Tenae - I know it hasn't been easy, painful at times, lost in the mess of life, but you shine like a star and make the darkness seem just like a backdrop. Our relationship is one of truth, "When we know what we know, there is no need to entertain what they think"

Life's lessons have embraced you and made you into the strong, beautiful character you are today, just know regardless of the journey, I love you and "I Got You"🩷

Love Ya'll....

To my brothers & sisters: Although we don't always see eye to eye, I do love you guys very much, collectively as well as, individually for different reasons. You all have always made me feel as if you were proud that I was your brother and that always made me proud to have you as my brothers & sisters in spite of all our imperfections. I have very fond memories of us as a family or whenever we'd all link up at mummy's, DJ Stagga and those 'Brenda' Lyrics, lol. Ringo and your humble teachings, Sonia with your 100mph everything lol, Yvette and those jokes about Ms. CrawCraw lol, I hope my books and achievements are something that I've done in my adult life to make you all proud. Love is Forever and a Day for you in my own special way!

Sted R.I.E.P: Just know that I love you, I feel you with me daily, piece of me left when you did, but I also found a part of me I never knew existed. It's all because of you, your still my driver, my reminder that tears come when they want so let them flow and laughter comes when it wants to hold onto the memories! I know your proud of all my accomplishments and had you been alive you'd have this book on your back seat, one in your blue CH4 bag, plus a box in your boot, sharing it with everyone you meet, beaming with pride saying "This is my little brother Tes", Sted your my Hero, love you 🧡

To my Dream Team, the mechanisms that make the machine work, the following I'm nothing without, when I speak of keeping my circle tight...this is it:

Nates, - I know you know the levels!!

Shelika - I know you know the levels too!!

Michelle Gayle – My Besty, My Pal, to think we stuck with each other for the rest of lives...Yipeeee. Thank you, I love you, Gucci Shoes or barefooted I got you x

Ezerine Manning – my cuzzy wuzzy, what would I really do without you, sometimes I feel like I don't show you enough, just know that in my hearts of hearts your in it, I'm truly grateful for your love, commitment, trust and support.

Coretta McCooty – My listening ear, thanks for always being there, open heart, open mind, open arms. Your spirit is 2nd to none, your mistakes and blunders always makes my day lol, love you always

Saf Giwa – Nothing has and never will change over the years. Can you believe from Frontline, Thasha & plaza to now My Book signings and the Ritz lol. My ride or die, my day start, sorry about the pic of us at the Pegasus but I could of gone worse and put the ones of you in your linen suits and dollar shaped earrings and big belcher chain looking like a female Shabba Ranks lol, I love your realness and forever keeping me humbled and grounded. I love you

Maxine Sutherland – My PA, Admin assistant, Stylist, Wardrobe, Chef....actually let's scrap the chef one lol. Thank you for your unconditional support with all my ventures, you've showed me what true loyalty is, and ill repay you by giving you 10% discount off the purchase price of this book lol, I love you x

Sydney Bartley, every aspect of my successful being, Kingship, belief, aware of my greatness, I owe to you! Thank you for guiding Sted who then in turn guided me. Thanks for your continued support, patience and belief in me.

Mr Grantley Haynes (I'll never forget your early input, mentorship and belief when at times I didn't believe in myself. Graham Winfield, Ray Coombes.

Grantley, your foundations helped me stand firm in the gideon, you showed me "The supreme art of war is to subdue the enemy without fighting".

Dr Beverly Lindsay OBE OD VLL - thank you for your unconditional guidance, love and motherly support, oh and the Fruit Punch & Cake lol.

Team AJN Birmingham - remarkable journey, remarkable family!

Dean Alexander - thanks for shining that torch when the lights went out, thanks bro.

My Forever's 👌🏽❤️

Mark Rowe, Nirena Jones, Sacha J, Avtar Obhi, Simone Cousins, Jeremy James (Jezza), Carla Gray, Suvers, Marlene Murray, Raj Bagry, Althea Peterkin, Jayde Pearson, Norma Clarke, Darryl James, Claire Rowe, Rosalee Morrison, Dr Beverly Lindsay, Trevor 'Gatecrash' Mcintosh, Eaton Gordon, Helen Platt, Finn Taylor, Joseph Mclean, Errol Lawson, Zauditu Ishuah, Mr Lloyd Blake, Tanya Donaldson, Omar (Rich Arab), Millicent Vernon, Andrea Oc (USA),....love you guys, you've seen the highs, the lows, the weak, the tears, the vulnerability, the stubborn, the arrogance, the ignorant, the jovial, the shit jokes, the best jokes, the even better jokes, my dancing, my Gregory impersonations, the every side of me and yet still you've never failed or given up on me, my success I owe to you, for holding me, keeping me humble, grounded and loving me for me!! If I've not mentioned you but you know you are significant then Thank you too x

A special thank you to Garnet Silk Jr (my brother from another mother), you appeared as if sent from the almighty, our coincidences run parallel, thank you for sharing my journey, sharing those thoughts, understanding my loss, understanding the highs and lows as we work tirelessly continuing to carve a legacy of those great who have passed, but still define our own legacy, our deep reasoning, your unconditional support, your projection of humbleness that slows me down when I'm on a mad one in Jamaica lol, Jah Guide!

An extra special thank you to all the team and those working behind the scenes at **DMJ Publishing**, thank you for believing in me and Investing in my dreams and my story. I'm truly grateful and look forward to a long-standing fruitful relationship.

I am thankful to all my family & friends who have helped and encouraged me over the years, I have no valuable words to express my thanks, but my heart is still full of the favours received from every person.

All praises to the most high one!

'Now I'm Famous'...do as your told and cater to my every need lol

"*If you ever think you're too small to be effective, you've never been in bed with a mosquito!*"....

WENDY LESKO
#MYTRUTH

STAFF

Agent: Nathan Wallen

PA/Publicist: Shelika Wallen

Accountant: Michelle Gayle

Designer: Darryl James (Scale DM)

Stylist/Advisor: Ezerine Manning

Administration/Assistant PA: Maxine Sutherland

Spiritual Advisor: Claire Rowe

Nutritionist/Advisor: Gloria: Wallen

Hair Technician/HD Kuttz: Michael Sutherland

Make-Up/Wardrobe: Jáy-da Pert

NOW I'M FAMOUS

USEFUL LINKS

National Domestic Violence Helpline
www.nationaldomesticviolencehelpline.org.uk

National AIDS Trust
https://www.nat.org.uk

Black Fathers Support Group
https://www.bfsg.org.uk

Homelessness support in England
https://www.homeless.org.uk

Cruse Bereavement Care
https://www.cruse.org.uk

Impact Solutions Group
http://impactsolutionsgroup.co.uk/

Mentoring
https://mentorloop.com/tomorrows-leaders/

Jamaica Basic Schools Foundation
https://www.jbsf.org.uk/

Prostate Cancer UK
https://prostatecanceruk.org/

Diamond Travel
http://www.diamondtravel.co.uk/

DMJ Publishing
authors@dmjpublishing.co.uk

Burton's Transportation Company Limited (Jamaica) Tour Agent & Transportation services
+1 (876) 849-5571

www.ingramcontent.com/pod-product-compliance
Lightning Source LLC
Chambersburg PA
CBHW040415100526
44588CB00022B/2836